Computer Applications in Management

COMPUTER APPLICATIONS IN MANAGEMENT

Edited by JOHN R. BIRKLE
and RONALD YEARSLEY

Foreword by LORD ROBENS

A HALSTED PRESS BOOK

JOHN WILEY & SONS
New York – Toronto

English language edition, except USA and Canada
published by
Associated Business Programmes Ltd
17 Buckingham Gate, London SW1

Published in the USA and Canada by
Halsted Press, a Division of
John Wiley & Sons Inc
New York

First published 1976

Library of Congress Cataloging in Publication Data

Computer applications in management.

    "A Halsted Press book."
    Includes bibliographies.
    1.   Business – Data processing – Addresses, essays,
lectures.   I. Birkle, John.   II. Yearsley, Ronald.
HF5548.2.C5837   1976   658'.05'4   76–5431

ISBN 0-470-15068-8

Printed in Great Britain by R. J. Acford Ltd
Industrial Estate, Chichester, Sussex

Contents

C. J. Hancock

Each part of the computer is described in easily understood
terms. Modern developments in the fields of data capture
and information distribution are described. Useful jargon words
are introduced and explained.

J. R. Birkle

The computer systems normally required by a management
team are introduced. They are concerned with the processing
of transactions between the company and its suppliers,
customers and employees. Resulting from the processing of
transactions are applications which provide information about
the state of the company and applications which assist with
controlling the day-to-day running of the company.

J. R. Birkle

There are some problems which are insoluble, but others for
which a computer's great memory, speed or mathematical

ability can be harnessed. Examples of the above types of problem are taken from the fields of critical path analysis, transportation, queuing theory and statistical modelling.

4. THE CONTROL OF THE FLOW OF MONEY 61
R. S. D. Stinton

This and the following chapters give practical ways in which the computer can be used to improve management perform-ance. Cash flow can be improved by collecting money from customers more quickly, reducing bad debts, controlling dis-counts both paid and received etc. The computer can assist by informing on key matters at the optimum time, answering queries on customers' and suppliers' accounts and speeding the methods of cash transfer.

5. THE CONTROL OF THE USE OF MONEY 85
I. Handyside

Money is a limited resource in great demand by all depart-ments. An integrated financial and management accounting system will provide the best form of control with the least clerical effort. A computer-based system will allow control over working capital to be exercised with the minimum of paper being produced, but with variations from budget being traceable to any level of detail.

6. INDUSTRIAL RELATIONS AND PERSONNEL MANAGEMENT 115
M. St Vincent

A computer system can be used to benefit employees as well as management. Personnel systems are based upon the need to maintain payroll records but can be extended to assist in career planning and personnel information retrieval. The privacy of the information is of great importance.

7. MANAGING THE CUSTOMER 141
B. Doouss

The computer's ability to handle detail makes it possible to treat each customer individually and, after assessing his preferences for discounts, products, promotions etc., to plan the optimum sales approach to him or decide to save money by leaving him alone. The profitability of each customer's account may be far from proportional to the sales turnover. A sales costing system can identify relative profitability.

8. PRODUCTION AND MATERIALS CONTROL 164

M. Thornley and D. Graham

This chapter describes the computer's role in making best use of production, labour and material resources. There are advantages and disadvantages in doing this. The advantages come from the great detail that the computer can handle, giving early warnings of shortages or surpluses of any resource. The disadvantages come from the inflexibility of such complex systems when management decides to make production changes beyond the scope of the original set of programs.

Acknowledgements

We wish at the outset of this book to acknowledge the help and encouragement we have received from our colleagues. Many have been in no way directly involved in this, but it was through their continual support and encouragement of our efforts that we undertook to extend this understanding of management technology. We wish also to thank our wives for their assistance in the preparation of typescripts.

In the editing of this volume our work has been greatly facilitated by the ready co-operation of all our contributors—busy men, many of them authors already in their own right. Their enthusiasm has once again emphasised the deep sense of frustration so many specialists feel when confronted with a lack of understanding of their subject on the part of general management. We should also like to acknowledge, on behalf of the authors, the debt we all owe to the originators of so many of the techniques and concepts discussed here. It is the nature of this volume that we have not included extensive references.

We wish also specially to thank Lord Robens, who has contributed the Foreword to this book.

Foreword

If every problem could be reduced to numbers, then the computer would provide the answers.

No business of any size today can be efficiently managed without the use of a computer.

Senior management need not know how the computer works, but only what it can do. Twenty-five years ago the computer was largely used as just another office machine doing the mediocre tasks of payroll, stock control etc. and its possibilities only guessed at. But the past quarter of a century has seen substantial improvement in the numbers of competent staff from analysts to operators, the provision of powerful and simple-to-use software and a considerable development of the hardware of data links, teleprocessing and multi-accessing.

These developments have been speedy in arriving and the gigantic advance in computer use and computer techniques in these recent years has provided management with the necessary tool to provide more efficient and economical management and a finer cutting edge in the competitive world of manufacturing industry, business and commerce.

The limiting factor is the capacity of management to use the computer to the best advantage.

Senior management can no more be expected to have a detailed understanding of, for example, the mathematical theory of linear programming or of some of the more sophisticated techniques that companies have developed for their own particular specialised requirement, any more than they can be their own lawyers, accountants, or any of the many qualified specialists, without which it is impossible to run a business effectively.

What management needs to know is just exactly what the computer can do to help him in his particular task.

I welcome this book because it answers this specific question. It is not technical in the sense of a textbook, it is a book written by computer experts for practical management use, and as a result will be found to be of inestimable value.

I believe, too, that as management now comes to recognise the computer as a tool of management, rather than a recording angel, companies will be able to maximise the use of their computers and utilise to the full this not inexpensive piece of equipment. The computer is a two shift animal, quite willing and able to work three.

Intelligent and adequate use of the computer can widen the horizon of management's ability far wider than anything that has happened so far in this century.

It enables management to have a greater capacity to deal in abstractions and concepts, enabling thinking to go far beyond conventional assumptions and the conventionally accepted limitations of creativity and innovation.

Modern computerised business systems can strip away the excrescences from the central task of management, which is innovation in all its forms.

Managers in the main, though familiar with the computer, still do not have sufficient knowledge of computers and mathematical techniques and the computer experts do not have the overall view of the business management situation.

The most effective use of the computer can only be achieved by a constant dialogue between managers, on the one hand, and model builders and systems analysts on the other. This leads to better operational researchers and one would hope the ideal, the managers who can use the computer.

That is what this book is all about. A practical book designed to help management in the more efficient use of the computer as an aid to management.

LORD ROBENS OF WOLDINGHAM

The Contributors: Biographical Notes

John Birkle graduated from Oxford, and entered the computer field in 1961 when he joined International Computers Limited. He installed several early computers and learnt the basic trade of systems analysis and programming. While with the Management Dynamics Group he was variously engaged in executive selection, consultancy at home and overseas and managing the consultancy activities of the Group. He has lectured to leading management groups and written for national and technical publications. He has also been a regular contributor to *Management Today*. He is now responsible for Data Processing and allied technologies with Courtaulds Limited.

Brian Doouss is a graduate of London University (B.Sc, M.Sc). He joined Unilever Limited in 1956 in T. Wall & Sons (Ice Cream) Limited, holding various production management positions involving direct control of labour. From 1962 until 1968 he was General Production Manager in Wall's Limited, responsible for all factories and a labour force of 2,000+. In addition he was Managing Director of Embisco Limited—the wafer and cone business—from 1964 to 1968. In 1968 he became Head of Management Services controlling all computer systems, programming, organisation and methods and industrial engineering support for the company and its subsidiaries, with complete control of production and distribution planning. In 1974 he was made Management Systems Controller, Birds Eye Foods, responsible for all computer and systems development and computer operations, which includes a central IBM 360/65 and 21 Nixdorf 880/45 on a linked network for all depot invoicing, stock and local statistics: budget approximately £3 million per annum. In 1975, in addition to being Management Systems Controller, he was appointed General Distribution Manager controlling the complete Birds Eye cold storage/transport and shop delivery operation with a budget of £26·5 million per annum.

Derek Graham was educated at Whitehaven Grammar School and Slough College. He is a Fellow of the British Production and Inventory Control Society and was a founder member of the London Chapter of the Society. He holds a post-graduate diploma in Management Studies and is an Associate Member of the British Institute of Management. He has published a number of papers and lectures on the use of computers in production control and other business applications.

He joined the Royal Air Force in 1948 and first started working with data processing equipment in the RAF in 1950. On leaving the RAF in 1960 he worked in the Planning Department of Johnson and Johnson at the time when that company introduced one of the earliest IBM 1400 computers in the United Kingdom.

In 1962 he joined ITT as Staff Consultant on computer applications for production control, leaving in 1966 to join the Rank Organisation in the Computer Controller's Office where he was concerned with the introduction of computers for production control, optical design, reservations and a number of accounting systems. He is now Deputy Controller of Central Management Services in the Rank Organisation.

Christopher Hancock was educated at Glasgow Academy and Trinity College, Dublin, where he read Economics, Mathematics and History. He joined Courtaulds Limited in 1969 as a member of the Central O & M Department but transferred after a year to one of the company's computer bureaux to gain a better appreciation of the technical and programming aspects of systems design. He has been responsible for the development and implementation of a number of major applications including an export sales accounting package and a multi-company credit control scheme. He is currently the manager of Courtaulds' Group Systems Department which provides an internal consultancy service on mainframe and visible record computer applications.

Ian Handyside, M.A.(Oxon.), entered data processing in 1952 when he joined Powers Samas Limited. After a period of designing and installing data processing systems in both the public and private sectors using mechanical and electro-mechanical equipment, he gained his first experience of electronic data processing through the use of the early electronic calculating machines and the Ferranti computers marketed by Powers Samas. With the merger of Powers Samas and Hollerith in 1959 to form ICT, Ian Handyside became deeply involved in the introduction of the ICT 1300 and 1500 ranges of computers. Then followed a period of eight years in consultancy in which he was concerned with computer feasibility and system studies, and was responsible for introducing systems using a variety of computers for processing financial control information. After a spell as data processing manager for a major group, which gave him practical management experience in planning and introducing computer-based financial control systems, he returned to computer consultancy work in 1974.

R. S. D. Stinton is an Accountant and now a Manager for Group Data Processing Services in the United Dominions Trust. He was first involved in computing in 1961 as a member of a team created to develop and implement large systems for the English Electric KDP10 machine installed by the Yorkshire Electricity Board, Leeds. He joined UDT in 1965 as Development Manager and was appointed as Data Processing Manager in 1970. He is responsible for establishing computer procedures to control a very large debtors' file with comprehensive MIS; the system runs on a twin IBM 370/145 supporting a range of on-line terminal applications.

Mike St Vincent was educated at Alleyn's School, Dulwich and at King's College, Newcastle. He has a degree in Mechanical Engineering having specialised in production engineering subjects.

He served a two-year post-graduate engineering apprenticeship before taking up an appointment in Work Study with an electrical motor manufacturer. Whilst there he undertook a complete survey of the paperwork systems and procedures as a special assignment and developed a taste for O & M. He was appointed the company's first O & M Officer and introduced unit record equipment in 1962; he was subsequently appointed Data Processing Manager.

He joined his present company, United Glass Limited, in 1964 as a senior analyst working on conversion from unit record equipment to the company's first computer. In 1967 he was appointed OR Manager and within one year had taken on responsibility for Programming and Computer Operations. In 1969 he took over as Group Management Service Manager and has been responsible for restructuring the management services function and introducing new EDP equipment utilising mini-computers linked to a central mainframe.

Since 1969 he has worked closely with group personnel and divisional administration to develop and implement group-wide payroll and personnel systems.

Michael Thornley first became involved with computers in 1959 after a period in professional accountancy. His initial experience concentrated on the application of large-scale computers and real-time systems. He has spent some six years as a management consultant and, for two years, was a director of the Diebold Group operating in the United States of America. He is now Management Services Controller of the Rank Organisation.

Ronald Yearsley is a Director of the Computer Consultants BIS Applied Systems Limited. He has worked with computers for over ten years. He was concerned with the early development of computer applications in the education and social services field. He has been involved with consultancy for over four years specialising in the personnel, training and organisational problems of the computer industry. His other positions include being an editor and joint owner of *Management Decision*, visiting lecturer at the Bradford University Business School, and editor of several widely acclaimed books on computers and management subjects. He is also a director of Business Intelligence Services Limited (BIS), BIS Brandon Limited and BIS-Deltak Limited and Darwinen Limited.

Introduction

Books about computers tend to describe the history and rapid evolution of these machines, and to stress their great power and speed. There is a great deal of information available about how to manage computers and professional computer staff, how to choose computers or bureaux or consultants. The difficulties of programming and of designing systems have also been widely publicised. Other volumes describe how computers carry out the routine chores of accounting, stock control and sales analysis —or manage data bases and information retrieval systems.

These subjects are of great importance to computer specialists, but though of passing interest to the professional manager they are not of real use to him. The manager wants to know 'How does all this help me?' 'If I spend all this money and employ these experts will I be any better as a manager, or will I just have a complicated system that I don't fully understand and which doesn't earn its keep?'

The objective of this book is to teach managers how computers can help them, and their colleagues, to perform better as managers. A manager's function is to contribute to the profitability of his company, directly or indirectly, by exercising his management skills in the control and application of a proportion of his company's resources. Computer systems can help him to do this.

In this book the responsibilities of management towards efficient use of the company's resources have been subdivided into making the best use of the company's money, materials, manpower, customers and production/service capacity. It is perhaps unusual to regard customers as a resource—but they are just as much a resource as are raw materials. They are in limited supply and tie up far too much working capital if not controlled carefully.

An unusual feature of this book is that the editors have approached several managers who are themselves applying computers in a variety of business environments, and have persuaded them to give their own time to write about their experiences, good or bad, and to describe how they have used computers to assist them as managers. The five chapters they have contributed describe how computer systems have assisted them, and other managers in their companies, to fulfil their responsibilities for:

1. Controlling cash flow, or in other words minimising the working capital. This assumes special significance in times of high inflation and high interest rates.
2. Using the available cash, or working capital, to best advantage and controlling its expenditure on whatever materials—animal, vegetable or mineral—very carefully.
3. Industrial relations. Providing both a service to and information about employees.
4. Customers. Using the available market as efficiently as possible and providing a service which will keep the customer coming back for more. The manager must also know if a customer is becoming unprofitable to him because of the selling cost, the distribution cost, the discounts allowed or demanded etc.
5. Production. Matching the resources of labour and machines against the cost and availability of materials, the cost of holding finished stock and the intangible benefit of customer service.

To assist in understanding computers and computer systems the editors have preceded these five chapters with three others which introduce computer equipment and computer systems in clear, everyday terms. The meaning of 'integrated systems' becomes very clear after reading Chapter 2 which puts the integrated system into its context of (a) all transactions between the company and others; (b) the analysis of these transactions to inform management about the state of the company in absolute terms and in relation to others; and (c) a planning and controlling system which assists management to make the best use of the resources available to them and to predict the requirement for the future resources (or the result of a lack of them).

The book is thus in two parts. The first describes the tools—the computer and the basic systems. The second part describes how to use these tools from a manager's point of view. The result is a highly informative insight into actual computer experience which will benefit any managers confronted by such questions as:

— is this computer being used properly?

— should we use a computer to help us with this problem?

— could we use a computer to help us to improve our, and therefore our company's, performance?

The book should also be studied by everyone engaged in selling computers and computer systems to management. Sales of these products are almost invariably conducted by persons with no experience or understanding of the computer user's outlook and problems.

CHAPTER 1

The Tools for the Job

By C. J. HANCOCK

It was only with the advent of the present decade that computers in industry really came to be appreciated for what they are—an additional management tool. Far from being an oracle or an expensive luxury, computers exist to provide managers with additional hands, memory and calculating power which they can use, together with their own abilities, to run their businesses in an efficient and profitable manner. Computers by themselves cannot replace managers nor can they make bad managers better. Indeed, it is no coincidence that some of those companies which have invested large amounts of capital in computer equipment fare no better in the market place than certain of their competitors with only a fraction of their computing resources.

This is a reflection not so much on the equipment or 'hardware' as on the manner in which it can be abused. Many computer installations are uneconomic and frequently serve as a smokescreen behind which the user attempts to conceal his own inadequacies as a manager. Hardware is extremely expensive and computer personnel are even more so. There is no doubt that in recent years technological development and the evolution of sophisticated operating procedures have enabled computer manufacturers to maintain a remarkably stable price structure in relation to the power and processing ability of their equipment. Unfortunately the benefits to industry are only small because hardware accounts for rather less than half the total costs incurred by the average computer installation. The acquisition of a computer, like any other piece of capital equipment, must be cost justified and its use must contribute towards the profitability of the company.

Although it is not essential for the manager to know precisely how a computer and its peripheral equipment operate, it is important that he understands the basic principles of a computer system and the functions of the various devices involved. In this way he is better equipped to appreciate both the possibilities and the limitations of his equipment with regard to the problems he wishes it to assist him with. In this chapter, therefore, we shall examine the various types of equipment available to the manager and briefly consider some of the ways in which they may be used.

THE BASIC CONCEPTS

Hardware is the generic name given to the physical components of a computer system as distinct from software which relates to the instructions or 'programs' performed by the system. Firmware and middleware are relatively new words which have crept into the computer professionals' jargon. Such words tend to increase the confusion of the interested layman and add to the mystique in which the industry delights to enshroud itself. For the purposes of this chapter it is sufficient to say that firmware and middleware refer to a specialised form of software developed by the manufacturers for the control and operation of peripheral devices.

Broadly speaking hardware comprises three types of equipment. Firstly, there are input and output devices which feed information to the computer for processing and produce the results in a usable form. Secondly, there are storage devices, or 'backing stores' as they are commonly called, which hold information until it is required for processing. Finally, at the heart of all computer systems, there is the central processor to which all the peripheral devices are connected. Acting on the instructions of a software program, the central processor takes data from an input device, retrieves the information it requires from the backing store and performs the requisite operations before returning the processed information to the backing store or direct to an output device (*see* Figure 1.1).

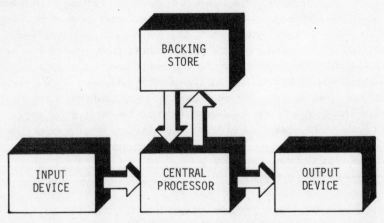

Figure 1.1   Basic System

A common sequence of events can be demonstrated by considering the processing of a company payroll. Details of clock numbers, hours worked at standard and overtime rates etc. are fed into the computer through a suitable input device. As the information or 'record' for each employee is read, the central processor retrieves from the backing store his name, hourly rates, cumulative pay and tax code. The amount to be paid is then calculated and the results output to a printer in the form of a payslip. At the same time, his cumulative pay is incremented by the appropriate amount and the 'updated' information is returned to the backing store to be processed again the following week. This cycle of operations is repeated for each employee until the payroll has been completed.

This is obviously a simplified account of the actual procedures involved but it serves to illustrate the use of backing stores. It does not, however, explain why backing stores are necessary and this can best be answered by considering the central processor in a little more detail.

CENTRAL PROCESSORS

The central processor incorporates its own storage medium or 'memory'. Until recently this consisted of small magnetised iron rings or cores strung together with fine wire to form a highly complex lattice capable of storing the program and working data currently required by the central processor. In later machines this method of construction has been superseded by pre-printed or solid state circuit boards which require much less space within the machine and are easier to repair or replace. We shall refer to this 'memory' as the core store to distinguish it from other forms of 'memory'. In addition to the core store the central processor also has a series of special stores or 'registers' collectively known as the arithmetic unit. This performs the various arithmetic and logical operations on data selected from the core store. The total operation of processing data through the system, initiating the required program instructions and directing the peripheral devices is carried out by the control section of the central processor. On all but the smallest computers this tends to be a software program called the Executive or Operating System which is permanently resident in the store, and is provided by the equipment manufacturer.

The size of a processor is measured by the amount of core store available and this can range from a few hundred characters in a small visible record computer to several million characters in the large machines commonly used by national and local government departments and the major industrial concerns. A character, in this instance, is the unit of measure which defines the computer's capacity to store alphabetic letters, numerals and symbols such as punctuation marks etc. Different manufacturers have adopted different units of measure such as 'bytes' and 'words'. The differences between these are not discussed here principally because they are largely technical and of little consequence to the user.

The method of measuring processing speeds also varies from one manufacturer to another due to differences in construction and the manner of operation. Most of the methods adopted revolve around the 'cycle time' which is measured in nanoseconds (one nanosecond is one thousandth of a millionth of a second) and which represents the amount of time taken to complete a fixed cycle of operations, e.g. locate and retrieve an item of data from the core store; calculate the sum of two numbers each of a given size etc. The speeds which can be achieved by modern computers are so phenomenal, however, that detailed comparisons are largely academic even to those people involved in the industry. To put processing speeds in their proper perspective, one should remember that in the minute or so it takes the average person to add 15 five digit numbers, a medium-sized computer could have accumulated over 100,000,000 such numbers. Furthermore, the computed sum will be correct which is more than can be said for the rather dubious arithmetic of a large number of people!

To use the potential processing speed of a computer, the information it is working on must be readily available. Unfortunately core store is extremely expensive and in consequence must be used as efficiently as possible. For example, it is obviously unnecessary to retain sales ledger information in the core store whilst one processes the payroll for 1,000 employees. It is even unnecessary when processing one man's wages to have resident in the core store the details of the remaining 999 employees. The solution, therefore, is to use other less expensive storage devices.

In practice, cheaper storage facilities are only available at the expense of an increase in the time taken to locate and retrieve information. The increased location time, known as the access time, caused by the physical movement of mechanical parts (not present in the core store), need not adversely affect the processing speed of the computer. For example, the program processing the payroll might request the retrieval of 25 employees' records at a time. Thus, by the time the central processor has dealt with the first 'block' of records, the next block has been found and retrieved. Other techniques adopted include the use of several storage devices at a time and 'multiprogramming' which involves the simultaneous processing of several different and independent programs in separate areas of the core store.

STORAGE DEVICES

Having examined the central processor and the need to supplement core store with backing store, we shall now consider some of the more common storage devices currently available. It is important that the manager appreciates the differences between them because the configuration of his computer and its peripheral devices will frequently affect what he does and how he does it, and sometimes mean that *it* is not worth doing at all.

MAGNETIC TAPE

All forms of storage device involve the recording of information on magnetically charged surfaces and the most familiar medium is probably magnetic tape which was introduced in the late 1950s as a much faster and more compact storage medium than the large files of punched cards it replaced. The storage potential of a modern 2,400-foot-long tape is in excess of 40,000,000 characters and the information held on it can be transferred into the core store at speeds ranging from 20,000 to 300,000 characters per second. Broadly speaking, magnetic tape decks operate in a manner very similar to that of a domestic tape recorder. One can record or write information onto a tape and one can play back or read information from a tape. One can also remove a reel of tape for storage purposes and replace it with another. Finally, when the information currently held on any tape is no longer required, it can be over-written and the tape used again for other applications.

Magnetic tape is available on reels of various sizes, and is also to be found in the small tape cassettes used in many visible record computer systems. These cassettes are in fact identical with those used in portable tape recorders—as many a computer manager has found to his cost! Another attraction of this versatile form of backing store, whether it be on reel or in cassette form, is that one does not need a computer to write information on it. Using a magnetic tape encoder, one can enter information through a keyboard similar to that of a typewriter and automatically record data onto a reel of tape. This can be removed and subsequently mounted on a tape deck attached to a computer which can then read and process the tape in the same way as any other tape file.

The most important aspect to remember about magnetic tape as a storage medium is that one has to begin at the beginning and read the tape until the last record stored on it has been reached. Furthermore, where more than one file is involved, each must be in the same sequence before processing can start. Amendments to such files are made by reading each record from a brought-forward file mounted on one tape deck and, after performing the necessary amendment, writing the updated record on a newly created carry-forward file mounted on a second tape deck. Items not being amended are simply copied from one to the other unless they are no longer required in which case they will be dropped completely. New transactions will be inserted in the carry-forward file in the correct sequence. If the amendments are held on cards or tape, this file must also be in the same sequence as the brought-forward master file for matching purposes or else the computer will be unable to find the record to which the amendment refers unless it scans up and down the tape every time.

Using magnetic tape obviously poses no significant problems for files such as a payroll master where the majority of records are updated or required whenever the file is used. In fact it has many attractions, particularly from a security point of view. One need only retain the brought-forward master file and the relevant amendments for each of a number of updates to create a cycle of files which can be used to reconstitute the latest file should it for any reason become damaged or lost. The cycle is perpetuated by always over-writing the oldest tape in the cycle by the output from each update. There is usually a minimum of three tapes involved in such a cycle (frequently referred to as the 'grandfather', 'father' and 'son') although more tapes can be incorporated according to the frequency of updating and the level of security required.

The serial nature of magnetic tape does, however, present problems when one wishes to find only a few records somewhere in the middle of a large sequential file or process records out of sequence. The solution to these problems lies in the use of direct access storage devices of which the most common is the magnetic disc.

MAGNETIC DISC

A magnetic disc pack comprises a number of flat discs stacked vertically and fixed to a central spindle which is rotated at high speed by the disc drive unit. With the exception of the two outermost surfaces, each disc surface within the pack incorporates a number of concentric tracks which store data. The data is located by 'read-write heads' of which there is at least one for each disc surface and sometimes as many as one for each track. For example, a 6-disc pack will contain 10 magnetised surfaces and be accessed by at least 10 read-write heads. The number of discs in a pack can range from a single-disc pack to an 11-disc pack capable of storing more than 800 million characters of information.

The first disc units to be introduced were known as 'fixed' discs because they could not be removed from the drives on which they were mounted. This was, to an extent, compensated for by their capacity to store a considerable amount of data and their ability to locate and retrieve that data very rapidly through the read-write heads which were usually static and mounted over each track. Although files could be loaded from magnetic tape and, after processing, unloaded back again for storage purposes, the most common use for fixed discs was probably for storing all the software required by the installation. Total flexibility of handling was not achieved until the development of the removable disc pack combined the versatility of magnetic tape with the accessibility of magnetic disc.

OTHER MAGNETIC STORAGE DEVICES

Magnetic drums were introduced in one of the early attempts to break the constraint of serial processing. The surface of a large horizontally mounted cylinder was divided into a number of tracks and over each track was mounted a fixed read-write head. Data was transferred to and from the magnetically charged surface of the cylinder while it revolved at approximately 3,000 r.p.m. In practice there are two drawbacks to this method of storing data and they probably account for the virtual disappearance of the magnetic drum from the manufacturers' product range. The first disadvantage is that data is only recorded on the surface of the cylinder which provides a limited storage capacity in relation to the volume of the device. The second is that although magnetic drums tend to have a faster average access time than magnetic discs, they are disproportionately more expensive. Generally speaking, drums are no longer an attractive commercial proposition and only a few small models are now in production.

Strips of magnetic tape loaded into a magazine form the basis of another type of storage device from which the data is retrieved by removing the appropriate strip and passing it round a spindle which acts as a read-write head. The strip is subsequently returned to its place in the magazine to complete a cycle of operations which takes roughly half a second. A similar device involving plastic cards measuring 7×3 in. is also available as a mass storage device although these magnetised cards, each containing nearly 13,000 characters of information, are more commonly found in small visible record computers. Neither of these devices offers any significant attractions over the more conventional types of storage equipment and it will probably be some time before there is a serious competitor to magnetic tape and discs. Prognostications concerning the future devolopment of computer technology are notoriously inaccurate, however, and one manufacturer is already exploring the possibility of using a laser beam to record information on the structural layers of a crystal.

INPUT DEVICES

Irrespective of the manner in which it is stored, all data must first be fed into the computer. The use of key-encoded magnetic tape has already been mentioned and it will be seen from this one example that even before data can be fed into the computer it must first be assembled into a suitable format on a medium which the computer can recognise and accept. In considering each input device, therefore, we shall also consider the input medium involved and the different ways in which it may be prepared.

'Garbage in, garbage out' has been a popular aphorism in the computer world for a long time and it expresses quite clearly the principle that unreliable input will produce unreliable results. The closer one can take the input medium to the source of the information, the smaller the numbers of errors will be and the manufacturers are constantly striving to bridge the gap between the creation of data and its subsequent processing. The input media and devices examined below will hopefully demonstrate the evolution of data entry to the point where direct or 'on-line' data entry systems are becoming quite commonplace in some sections of the commercial market, e.g. banking, airline ticket reservation, automated warehousing etc.

PUNCHED PAPER TAPE EQUIPMENT

Punched paper tape was the first input medium to be developed for computers and for a long time many used it not only to accept raw input data but to load their software programs as well. Many small visible record computers continue to load programs in this manner rather than become involved in the expense of additional backing store or suffer the constraint of being able to perform only one permanently loaded program. Information is recorded by punching rows of holes along an inch-wide strip of paper tape which is wound onto a large reel for storage purposes. There are ten rows punched in every inch of tape giving a 1,000-foot-long tape a nominal storage capacity of 120,000 characters. Each numeral from '0' to '9', each letter of the alphabet and each of the special symbols such as punctuation marks etc. is denoted by a unique combination of holes and each row of holes will store one such uniquely defined character.

The maximum number of holes which can be punched into any one row varies from five to eight according to the coding system involved. Nowadays, the most frequently used codes rely on an eight-hole system in which the first seven holes identify 128 letters, numerals and symbols while the eighth hole is used for checking and character control purposes. Also present in each row is a smaller hole known as the 'sprocket-hole' which coincides with a small toothed drive wheel in the paper tape reader. This method of mechanically feeding the tape is only practicable on slow readers because the drive wheel tends to rip the tape at high speeds. On the faster paper tape readers which read the tape at approximately 2,000 characters per second, it is friction-fed through rubber rollers and the punched holes are sensed photo-electrically rather than physically by flexible brushes.

Paper tape is punched by a device incorporating a keyboard similar to that of a typewriter or the magnetic key tape encoder mentioned earlier. The operator reads information from a source document, which could for example be an employee's clock card or a sales invoice, and types it on the keyboard to be converted into the appropriate combination of holes in the paper tape. After a batch of input has been completed, it is normally checked or 'verified' to ensure that no errors have occurred in the course of copying the information from the source documents. Verification is accomplished by 'reading' the newly punched tape on a second machine called a verifier and punching a second tape from the same source documents. As each character is keyed, it is compared with the equivalent character in the original tape and any discrepancy will prevent the punch and the keyboard from functioning until the error has been corrected. To avoid the risk of errors being repeated, it is customary to employ a different operator for verification although errors caused by untidy, misleading or badly written source documents may still go undetected.

The use of paper tape for computer input has the attraction that it is inexpensive, reasonably fast and involves equipment which is simple and easy to maintain. The tape is also compact enough to be readily portable or, if time and distance are significant factors, it can be transmitted over standard telephone lines using the appropriate communications equipment. Its disadvantages are the obvious problems of error correction, the cumbersome manner in which it is prepared and the remarkable ease with which even an experienced operator can feed it into a computer upside-down, back to front, spliced the wrong way etc. The more serious problems of manual preparation and error correction are not present when paper tape is produced automatically as a by-product from another machine and it is in this area that paper tape continues to be a popular form of computer input.

Many companies use invoicing machines or small visible record computers to produce sales invoices and a large number of these machines incorporate paper tape handling facilities. Using this type of equipment, one can raise a batch of invoices and, at the same time, automatically produce a length of paper tape containing all the required information correctly punched from each invoice. The tape will normally be terminated by a control record containing the total value for the batch which has been accumulated by the machine to avoid a dependence on manually computed totals for control purposes. Once it has been removed from the machine it can immediately be used as input to a computer for invoice analysis, posting to the sales ledger etc. This approach eliminates the risk of manual punching errors and saves the time and costs incurred by data preparation.

Unfortunately, errors will still occur if the machine operator incorrectly enters the customer's name and address, the product description or the unit price when completing an invoice. A common solution to this problem is to maintain two files of cards, one each for the customers and the products. On each card will be typed a customer's name and address or a product description plus unit price. The same information will also be punched into an inch-wide strip down one edge of the card as though it were paper tape. These edge-punched cards are fed through a special paper tape reader on the invoicing machine as though they were tape and the information contained in the strip will automatically be typed onto the invoice and faithfully reproduced in the output paper tape.

If, in this situation, the name and address cards were large enough, they could be used as ledger cards to record the details of the customer's account and the product cards could similarly be used to record stock movements. The permutations which can be achieved in this way are endless and many of them involve a free-standing visible record computer system which does not need to produce paper tape for use as input to a larger computer. It is also true to say, however, that several large organisations operate these systems in remote units and still produce output tape to be processed and analysed by a computer located in the organisation's head offices to satisfy the latter's need for management information.

In conclusion, paper tape is cheap and ideally suited as a means of data transfer from one machine to another. Although it is also produced as output by other machines which have been designed to overcome the problems of manual data preparation, it is tending to be superseded by the more flexible medium of magnetic tape. For this reason we shall consider these machines and other less conventional methods of generating computer input in the context of magnetic tape but only after examining the other traditional input medium—punched cards.

PUNCHED CARD EQUIPMENT

Punched cards were already being used at the turn of the century to store information which could subsequently be sorted, collated, mechanically extracted and used to generate reports on the first tabulators and simple accounting machines. The potential of punched cards both as a file storage medium and as a form of input was quickly realised and many of the early computers were built round the use of cards as a crude form of serial backing store. Although these card computers tended to disappear with the introduction of magnetic storage media, the 80-column punched card is the most common form of computer input to this day. There are in fact other sizes of cards with capacities ranging from 21 to 96 columns but none has experienced the same universal acceptance or stood the test of time so well. This point is amply borne out by the 96-column card in particular which is currently available from most of the major manufacturers. It is approximately one third the size of a standard 80-column card, contains 20% more data and can be processed much faster. Yet despite these obvious advantages, it has failed to make any significant impact on the market.

A normal 80-column card measures $7\frac{3}{8} \times 3\frac{1}{4}$ in. and each column contains 12 possible punching positions. Using the Hollerith code which was perfected in the late 1880s, combinations of holes can be punched into each column to identify numerals, alphabetic letters and symbols etc. The technique is obviously similar to that used in punching paper tape except that punched cards have the added refinement that the holes in each column can be 'interpreted' by a device which decodes the holes and prints the appropriate character at the top of the column. Cards may be interpreted by a machine specifically installed for the purpose or by some of the more expensive card punching machines. Card punches utilise a keyboard and operate in much the same way as paper tape punches and magnetic key tape encoders. The verification of punched cards is also similar to that of paper tape except that a second set of cards is not punched because any single card found to be in error can readily be corrected or replaced by a single new card.

This ability to correct and replace cards easily makes the 80-column card a very simple medium to handle and, because it is not subject to the serial processing constraints of paper tape or magnetic tape, it is extremely flexible and popular. Generally speaking, one card is used to contain one record of information which could be anything from the details on a sales invoice to a line from a software program. The information is stored in the card by dividing it into a number of separate areas or 'fields' each containing a pre-defined number of adjacent columns. Different jobs will obviously require different combinations of fields and field sizes and the software program which reads the cards in for a specific job will incorporate a layout of the card so that it can locate and identify the fields it is required to process.

The main drawback to this concept of a unit record whose contents are infinitely variable is that each card contains a fixed number of columns which will obviously be insufficient for some applications. The information to be recorded can of course be allowed to overflow onto a second or third card etc. but this immediately presents one with the problem of a pair or set of cards which, although not physically connected, must be kept together and in the right sequence. At the same time it is also inefficient if one uses only a few columns of the last card in the set. Not only is the storage capacity of the card under-utilised but computer processing time is wasted because the card reader will take the same amount of time to read the card whether it is full of data or completely empty.

In an attempt to use cards more efficiently, some installations organise their work in such a way that the card layouts for jobs with a small amount of data required on each input record, when overlaid on a single card, carry across the card and do not overlap. This means that the same card can hold data for a number of totally unrelated jobs and a batch of similarly punched 'spread' cards need only be fed through the input card reader once irrespective of the number of different jobs involved. The theory of spread cards is rather more attractive than its practical application, due largely to the need for adequate batch control and audit trail procedures. As with all other areas of data processing, it is important that the *modus operandi* of a computer installation serves the best interests of its users and not of those who are responsible for running it.

The punching and subsequent verification of cards is less tiresome than that of paper tape but errors still occur and of course data preparation still takes time and costs money. The solution developed using paper tape was to punch it automatically as a by-product from a visible record computer application such as invoicing. From a practical point of view one can produce punched cards in exactly the same manner but because card punches are several times the price of paper tape punches this is not normally a cost effective solution. A more frequent situation involving cards is to use them as a 'turn round' document and this can be achieved in two ways.

The first is concerned with maintaining card files processed and punched by a computer and the most common applications are those which involve one card for each item or unit record such as sales accounting and stock recording systems. For example, when items are posted to a computerised sales ledger, the computer can be directed to punch a card for each new transaction. The cards are then manually filed by account until a payment is received at which point the card representing the relevant invoice is selected from the file and submitted to the computer for reprocessing as a settled item. The approach is ideal when there are relatively small volumes involved but the ability to operate such a system efficiently is quickly lost when the volumes increase. The problems of storing and handling thousands of cards, reconciling a payment which is made 'on account' and not against a specific invoice or invoices etc. conspire to create a situation which becomes increasingly difficult to control.

The second uses a fundamentally different approach known as mark-sensing. A specially printed 80-column card is marked in a selection of pre-determined fields by a graphite-based pencil or fibre-tip pen. The card, which can also be punched, is then fed through a device which senses the marks and either converts them into actual holes or punches the contents of the card into paper tape. The technique is particularly useful in the areas of production control and work-in-progress reporting. For example, operatives mark details of their department together with the date and the quantity and quality of the goods processed on a card which contains a pre-punched product code and customer's order number. The completed cards can be read and punched into paper tape daily to be processed and analysed overnight by a computer. Despite a fairly active marketing drive by the manufacturers in the late 60s, the idea failed to become accepted commercially due probably to the unfounded belief that the cards could not be kept sufficiently clean but would instead become contaminated by graphite grease and dirt. This would in turn corrupt the sensing of the marked data which would result in the production of unreliable results.

Despite the shortcomings outlined above, punched cards are still the most flexible form of computer input and virtually all mainframe computers have an input card reader which operates by photo-electrically sensing the holes as the cards are fed in. Reading speeds vary according to the make and model of the card reader but the maximum is currently in the region of 1,500 cards per minute. Assuming the cards are full of data, this permits an input speed of 2,000 characters per second which is comparable to a high speed paper tape reader. These speeds are still slow, however, in relation to those achieved by magnetic devices and as a result it is common practice on all but the smallest computer systems to read the cards into the machine and record the contents straight to the backing store. Because this can be performed while the computer is processing another job, there is no time wasted and when the input data is required for processing it can be read at high speed from the backing store.

It is the development of techniques like this which has overcome the problems presented by the vastly differing speeds at which the various types of peripheral equipment operate. In fact the old adage that a computer is only as fast as its slowest peripheral device has little validity in these days of sophisticated operating systems and multiple input/output devices.

MAGNETIC TAPE EQUIPMENT

We have already seen that magnetic tape encoders operate in much the same way as card and paper tape punches although an encoded magnetic tape is a far faster input medium than cards or paper tape. Despite the obvious advantages of magnetic tape as a medium, magnetic tape encoders are not used for conventional data preparation as often as one might expect due probably to the relatively high cost of the equipment. They are, on the other hand, frequently used in conjunction with communications devices which facilitate the data preparation of information at a remote site. Input data is first encoded onto magnetic tape which is then transmitted to a computer for processing. Errors which are detected by the computer can be transmitted back to the remote site for correction using the source documents which are generated and stored locally.

To facilitate error correction, the equipment at the remote site is often supplemented by a small printer. Error reports continue to be produced by the main computer but instead of being output to a printer, they are written on magnetic tape. The tape is then transmitted to the remote site in the same way as the rejected input transactions where it is either printed as the telephone transmission is received or recorded on a tape encoder for printing afterwards. Because magnetic tape can be processed at extremely high speeds it is ideally suited for data transmission and as a data transfer medium from one high speed machine to another. The limiting factor on the speed of data transmission is neither the tape nor the transmission equipment but the quality of the telephone lines. In fact most organisations use their own private telephone systems or special lines rented from the Post Office rather than depend on the public network.

The ability to edit and correct simple data preparation errors before the updating and processing of files begin is obviously of great benefit, particularly to remote users. Corrections for jobs which have a weekly update, for example, need not be held back until the next run and management reports contain all the information submitted to the computer and not just what it has processed. For these reasons, many systems require that the editing of input data is carried out as a separate function on the computer and before the main processing for a job commences. It would be of even greater benefit, however, if no editing were required at all and only error-free input were submitted for processing. This would not only save processing time and simplify control procedures for all users but also reduce the amount of transmission required to and from remote users.

This ideal situation can be achieved by providing a data preparation device with sufficient processing power to detect simple errors and check that specific input fields are numeric or fall within a specified range etc. To provide each data input operator with such facilities would be extremely expensive and the normal procedure is to connect the required number of keyboards to one small processor. Data is keyed in by the operators and edited by a software program according to the layout of the input record and the requirements of the system concerned. All accepted data is recorded on a disc which is connected to the processor and is common to all the keyboard terminals involved. If any errors are detected, they are displayed on a small visual display unit which looks rather like a television screen located in front of each operator near the input keyboard. As input data is entered through the keyboard it is displayed on the screen and, if it proves to be unacceptable, an error message explaining the cause of rejection will appear and no further data will be accepted from that operator until the error is rectified.

When a batch of input data has been completed or when the disc is full, the accepted information is transferred to magnetic tape which can then be removed and, after transmission if necessary, reloaded onto the computer for processing. Thus the approach combines the efficiency of a high speed input medium with the benefits of 'clean' or error-free input data for an unlimited number of jobs. As one would expect, this form of 'key-to-disc' system is not cheap but an increasing number of companies now feel that the savings in processing time plus an improvement in their operating efficiency make it a worthwhile acquisition. Although key-to-disc systems are available with as few as three keyboard terminals or 'keystations', it is more common to see half a dozen or so attached to one processor. This is because the cost of a keystation is small in relation to the processor and the larger installations can therefore handle much greater volumes of data for only a small increase in the equipment costs.

Magnetic tape, whether it be on reel or in cassette form, can be produced by most visible record computers and other off-line data preparation devices. Although it is more expensive, it is tending to replace punched cards and paper tape as a medium to be produced as an automatic by-product from these machines because it is much faster, requires less intermediate handling and is best suited to data transmission. Most of the techniques and machines designed to eliminate data preparation by automatically encoding source data onto a medium acceptable to a computer now rely mainly on magnetic tape as a medium for data transfer. Document readers are a typical example of this type of equipment and they can be divided into two categories according to the technique used in completing the input document. Firstly there is optical character reading or OCR which requires the reader to recognise pre-printed characters which have been typed by an ordinary typewriter using a special character set. The technique is restrictive, however, and considerably more expensive than the second approach which is optical mark reading or OMR.

OMR is a more refined method of the mark-sensing we referred to when discussing punched cards. A sheet of paper is divided into a specified number of lines and each line is divided into a number of fields rather like a punched card. Each field contains a number of boxes which have a pre-defined value and the document is used by putting a horizontal mark or bar through the required boxes. The completed document is then fed through a document reader which scans each line and encodes the marks onto magnetic tape or into paper tape. When processed by the computer, the encoded marks are converted to the pre-defined values and subsequently handled like any other form of input data.

A company payroll is an excellent example of a worthwhile OMR application. To overcome the problem of punching and verifying large amounts of data in a short space of time, the computer is used to generate a turn-round document for each employee by printing his name and bar-marking the matching key details such as clock number, department number etc. These documents are then passed to the wages office where they are matched against the relevant clock cards. The details of hours worked, overtime etc. are bar-marked onto the turn-round form and when all have been completed the total input documentation for 2,000 employees can be fed through the OMR reader in about an hour. Permanent amendments to the employees' details on the master file can be made using a similar technique although it is best suited to the simple numeric coding of values, quantities etc. For this reason, OMR should be considered as a supplement to conventional data preparation procedures rather than as a replacement.

OUTPUT DEVICES

There is, in effect, only one output device which produces a permanent hard copy record of what the computer has processed and that is the printer. There can be few computer installations in the country which do not have some form of printer, yet despite the variations in construction and methods of operation, they can all be classified as either 'line' printers or 'character' printers. Line printers, as the name implies, print one complete line of data at a time and they are rated at speeds in the range 90 to 1,800 lines per minute. The actual speed of any printer will in fact vary enormously according to the maximum possible length of the print line, the number of characters which are available to be chosen from for printing and the software program controlling the printer at the time.

Character printers operate like typewriters and print one character at a time. This type of printer is usually to be found as an integral part of most visible record computers or as a remote terminal attached by a communication link to a computer. The slower character printers operate at 10—50 characters per second and normally incorporate a spherical type head. The faster printers operate at about 120 characters per second and tend to use a matrix print head. The printed characters for these machines are formed by a matrix of fine pins each of which can be raised or lowered to make patterns of dots corresponding to letters, numerals etc. There are few character printers which achieve actual print speeds in excess of 150 characters per second because beyond this point it is more efficient and more economic to use a small line printer.

To overcome the problems of slow input devices, we saw how it was a common policy to write input cards to backing store while the computer was processing another job. Because even the fastest line printers are also slow in relation to processing speeds, a similar practice is often employed with output reports and this helps to balance the lengthy processing jobs with minimal print requirements against the small job which generates a considerable amount of paper.

Although one can store reports on magnetic tape indefinitely and use them time and again, this is not an economic use of tape nor is it very efficient in terms of the area required for storage. The use of micro-film for storing general office and company records has been quite common for many years now but it is only very recently that Computer Output on Microfilm/fiche, commonly known as COM, has come to the fore as a viable alternative to paper as an output medium.

This has been assisted partly by the developing technology of COM and partly by the escalating costs of paper. Microfiche in particular has experienced a remarkable expansion since it became possible to load a magnetic tape containing one or more reports onto a COM processor and produce fiche immediately. No paper is involved at any stage and there is no limit to the number of copies which can be produced. One thin plastic sheet of microfiche will hold up to 270 full pages of computer print-out and the fiche can be loaded into a viewer and enlarged for reading on a screen 14 × 11 in. Some fiche viewers have a small photocopier attached which can be used to reproduce whatever is displayed on the viewing screen. Generally speaking, COM saves storage space, reduces paper and handling costs and in terms of the viewing equipment can be obtained fairly cheaply. Unfortunately, the cost of a COM processor is prohibitively expensive and most users currently use the bureau facilities offered by some of the larger banks and commercial organisations who have COM for their own internal systems and sell what spare time they have on their processors to other users.

ON-LINE TERMINAL PROCESSING EQUIPMENT

All the techniques and equipment considered so far have been concerned with improving the quality of input data, taking it from its source of origin and feeding it into the computer as quickly as possible. Data preparation and communications have been 'off-line' in the sense that the devices involved are not physically connected to the computer and the transfer of data is subject to input cut-off times, processing schedules etc. Even when the data is finally presented to the computer there are delays while it is processed, printed and distributed. Despite this, the concept of taking a batch of input data, applying the necessary control procedures and then waiting while it is input and processed works perfectly well for the majority of computer users most of the time. Furthermore, if the computer happens to break down for a couple of hours the rest of the organisation is not brought to a standstill.

Conversely, on-line computer systems frequently involve an unhealthy dependence by the user on his equipment and there are, in addition, a lot of misconceptions involved, many of which emanate from the misguided enthusiasm of the user's own systems staff. On-line data entry is frequently referred to as 'transaction processing' because the emphasis is normally on processing a single transaction through a system at a time rather than the conventional batch. The procedures involve the entering of data through the keyboard of a suitable terminal device which, by definition, must be both an input device to enter data and an output device to receive an acknowledgement of input or an answer. Terminals range from the simple low speed teletype which comprises a keyboard and a 30-character per second printer to a high speed visual display unit or VDU with a screen capacity of 24 lines containing 80 characters each.

Another type of terminal is the versatile visible record computer. It is, in this context, often referred to as an 'intelligent' or 'interactive' terminal because it can perform a preliminary amount of processing prior to accessing the main computer. This helps to reduce the main computer's processing requirements which in turn speeds up the response to the terminal. This approach has been adopted by some of the major banks who have installed visible record computers in every branch to input each day's transactions to the main computer. The information is edited and put into format by the visible record computer before being transmitted to the main computer for immediate updating onto the customers' accounts. The terminals can also be used to receive and print the details of any customer's account as soon as the appropriate request has been initiated.

The essence of being on-line is that, through the medium of the terminal, one has access not only to the computer's backing store but to the central processor as well. In fact given the appropriate software, there is very little one cannot do. For example, if one uses a VDU to update a company's sales ledger with all the relevant transactions as and when they occur, the ledger will be continually up to date. By entering a suitable instruction code and a customer's account number the user can, in effect, initiate his own processing and the central processor will retrieve the customer's data from backing store and display the latest information on the user's VDU whether it be in the next room or in the next county.

Depending on the equipment involved and the size of the files to be interrogated, a simple transaction like this will be completed in about 2−3 seconds. The facility also exists to attach a small printer to a VDU so that at any time the contents of the screen may be reproduced in a hard copy form.

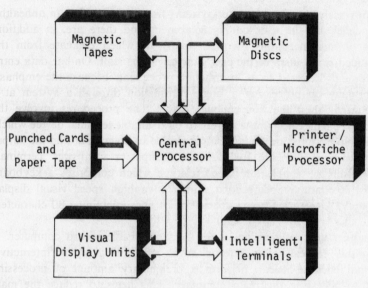

Figure 1.2   Large System

Figure 1.2 shows, diagrammatically, a large computer configuration. That real benefits can be gained from a system of this type is beyond dispute and the potential applications are virtually unlimited. Companies are continually developing new and different uses although the traditional problem areas of production recording, stock control, sales accounting and credit control are still the most common applications. On a more practical footing, however, it must be said that the implementation of real-time systems is extremely expensive and almost invariably costs twice as much as expected. Although the user may benefit from the rapidly produced information, it should be recognised that it is information at a price and unless it has made a positive contribution to the company's profits, the price is too high. The final criterion in all cases should be one of cost justification.

CHAPTER 2

The Manager's Day-to-day Applications

BY J. R. BIRKLE

WHAT IS THE COMPUTER'S JOB?

Have you ever looked round at the successful men in your company and tried to assess which are the high-fliers and which are the steady work-horses? I expect so; it is one way of assessing one's own prospects and we all do that from time to time. Have you noticed which category makes use of information—be it computer-produced or manually culled from orders, invoices or stock sheets? It is not the high-fliers. Information gets in their way, they are the 'don't confuse me with facts' men. They have learnt that when they want information quickly it is not available, or if it is, then it has been produced in a rush and contains errors. So they work on intuition, on a knowledge of people and on confidence in their ability to sort something out later if anything goes wrong.

Computers are not compatible with the intuitive manager for one very simple reason: they have no mercurial capacity whatsoever and will continue plodding in the direction they have been given, until some-body painstakingly alters their course. Very dull but very useful. Protect us from a company full of high-fliers you will be saying—somebody has to do the work!

In this chapter we are going to start developing the theme of how a computer can be made into one of the workhorses of the management team. Lesson one is recruitment. You may recruit a high-flier on the basis that he is obviously a good man, straight from business school, 'come in and learn the business' and so on, knowing that a niche will be found for him later. You don't recruit a workhorse like this at all. You define the job that has to be done, then you find someone with the right experience and teach him, within his capabilities, how to do the job you have defined. Planning the recruitment of your computer is very similar—the secret is in defining all the work that has to be done before starting to look for the computer. If you are unsure of making a total definition of the computer's job, then don't think you can learn fast enough to keep pace once it has arrived. It is much better to go to a bureau and do *your* learning there.

The most useful, which means cost effective, computers are invariably those where the management team have worked out a complete objective well in advance. This objective may be a single application such as the capture of customer-order data, the control of stocks, the booking of airline seats or control of a production unit. The objective may be much wider, such as performing all the accounting, stock-keeping, production and payroll applications for the company. The important point is that the full definition of the computer's role must be decided in advance of development of any one application.

The least successful installations are those where the objective keeps shifting. First of all, perhaps, the payroll is processed, then spare capacity at the end of the week is used for printing invoices. Then someone decides to print work-tickets on Monday mornings. Sales ledger suddenly becomes a necessity, 'it's the only way we will collect the money owed to us', but the computer isn't quite powerful enough and another bit of equipment has to be tacked on.

Such a pattern of *ad hoc* development is very common in smaller companies, but the mistake is never made again. Within two or three years it is 'back to the drawing board' and a comprehensive systems design is written down, discussed and agreed.

In this chapter are described, briefly, those applications which should be considered for inclusion in an overall systems plan which will result in promotion of the computer to management status. The applications are those which are susceptible to computer assistance in any commercial enterprise which buys materials, does something to them and sells the finished product. These applications are called 'day-to-day' because they assist management with the necessary paperwork and information for running a business. In the next chapter we shall examine how, having taught the computer to cope with all the day-to-day applications, it can be taught not only to collect, sort and display the information with which management can improve its methods of controlling, planning, forecasting and decision-making, but also how to do some problem-solving itself.

This separation of the role of a computer into that of 'doing' and that of 'informing' mirrors the role of the accountant who, in all probability, will have responsibility for the computer in small and medium-sized companies. For a long time the accountant's role was considered to be purely executive; his job was closely defined by the owners of the business and his function was merely to follow this job definition. As business became more complex, however, the expertise of the accountant in handling and interpreting figures made him a necessary member of the management team. This is what happens to a properly used computer! It is so efficient at marshalling figures that its use can be extended to interpreting the figures so that management can take more effective decisions and monitor the results of those decisions.

Unfortunately the computer, left to itself, can do nothing—it is as much use as an accountant who is permanently asleep. Introducing the computer to the way the company works, teaching it to do the closely defined part of its work and preparing it for its sophisticated information processing role is the job of the systems and programming team. Programming is the exact instruction of the computer in the tasks defined for it by management and interpreted by the systems analyst. We shall not be considering the programming of the computer, but will confine ourselves to the tasks that we want it to carry out—the 'systems' as they are called.

SYSTEMS

The art of computer systems design is to make the computer do a specific task in a simple, economical way and to make provision for the system to be adapted, as the needs of the organisation change. It is also necessary to allow the computer system to share the files and transactions it processes with other systems where overlap occurs. Lastly it is necessary to provide a means of assembling information in a concise, useful form in response to queries from other members of the management team.

This last requirement is the most difficult because it is open-ended. Perplexed systems designers will usually begin by stating that the requirements of each system must be precisely stated. This makes his life much easier but leads to a much less useful system. A computer which is rigid about the questions it will accept and the answers it gives will never join the management team. The variety of questions that managers have to answer and the decisions that they have to take is such that the information they need at their finger-tips must change from decision to decision and from day to day. If you ask a manager what information he needs about stocks or staff or customers he will only be able to tell you about the last problem he had to deal with—not the next one. The system which the computer is instructed in must give a quick answer to predictable questions and be capable of producing an answer to other (answerable) questions after a reasonably short space of time. That is to say after someone has interrogated the information held within the computer in a sensible way. The worst kind of system just prints out everything on miles of rather expensive paper in the hope that someone will be able to find the parts of the answer they need somewhere within it.

In order to make a computer into one of the management team—the manager in charge of information in fact—it is a good idea to give it as much information as possible as otherwise it will be totally ignorant on some subjects. We want it to be able to take materials ordered into account when it tells us about stock availability. We want it to take production capacity into account when it tells us about the date a particular order will be met. This is what is meant by an 'integrated' system.

All the information about the day-to-day operation of the company comes from the systems illustrated in Figure 2.1.

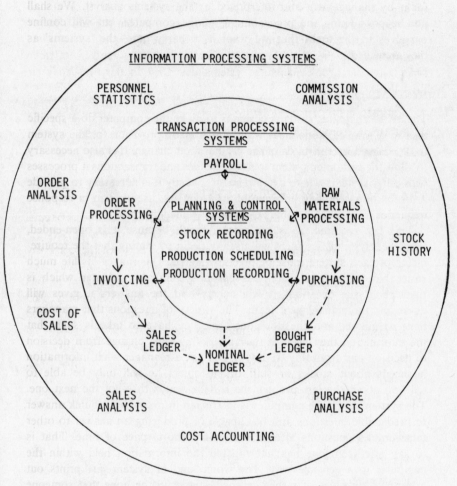

Figure 2.1   The Relationship of the Three Basic Types of System

In any particular company the importance of some of these systems will be greatly magnified in relation to the others. The production system may in some companies be based upon very complicated formulae or upon vital recipes—the value of the computer being in minimising the cost of meeting outstanding orders from the raw materials available. In another company we may find the production system being comparatively simple, but that minimising the value of finished stock is top priority.

It is not intended that all these systems should be described in this book. They are well known in outline anyway, and are the stock-in-trade of any able systems analyst. What is important is that they should all be considered as a whole at the planning stage so that they fit together neatly and do not, for example, require separate files to hold identical information. As the diagram shows, computer systems may be of three types plus the problem-solving systems described in the next chapter: these three types are:

1. Transaction processing systems
2. Information processing and analysing systems
3. Planning and control systems

TRANSACTION PROCESSING SYSTEMS

Transaction processing is the source of the data for the other systems. A transaction is simply the movement of goods or money or services from one point to another within the company or between the company and another party—who might be an employee, a customer or a supplier. The term transaction processing, although a perfect description of this class of system, must be used with care. It has become commonly used to describe any form of computer processing in which each transaction is processed separately, via a terminal, as opposed to 'batch' processing, in which transactions are batched together and processed periodically.

It is not intended to describe the individual systems in this class. They are very well known, and come under a variety of names of which the following are a typical set:

Invoicing

Sales Ledger

Materials Processing

Purchasing

Purchase Ledger

Payroll

Salaries

These systems are, by definition, the first to be 'computerised'; they will not make the computer into one of the management team—only into a super-clerk.

The most important point to watch for is that *all* transactions are processed, if the computer is to progress to being manager of information. It may not be necessary or economic to process each transaction in detail, but in summary form each one should be represented. Such transactions as sales to staff are often overlooked, but regretted later when a complete stock control system is required.

INFORMATION PROCESSING AND ANALYSING SYSTEMS

We shall now assume that the basic files and functions of the transaction processing systems have been designed and we are going to look at information processing and analysing systems. These are usually known as 'sales analysis', 'personnel statistics', 'customer history' etc. but these are all different labels for the same thing—trying to print the information which has been collected by transaction processing systems in a useful way, and with assumptions made about what is going to be useful and what is not. It is our opinion that this type of print-out should be kept to the absolute minimum, particularly as paper costs have risen so sharply. The objective should be to have a method of presenting the information when it is required, and limited to only what is required. For instance, if we want to know which customers are buying a particular product, how much is in stock and how much is scheduled for production in the next three months, we shouldn't have to print out or wade through any other information about other customers or products. To design for this kind of flexibility, we must understand more about information processing.

Information Processing

'Information processing' refers to the various processes involved in storing a large amount of information in computers (stored, of course, in the form of 'data'), and making it possible for people to draw on the information as and when they need it. This is where it differs from 'data' processing. While data are values of symbols which can be formulated for programs to operate on, 'information' consists of data which can be used for answering a question, solving a problem or making a decision. Isolated data items are not informative unless they are fitted into a frame of reference or experience which can be called on for answering questions. Data processing conventionally provides standard answers to pre-set questions programmed in detail, one by one. An information processing system draws on a store of information as its users have problems—just as people are continually calling on the experience and knowledge stored in their minds. In other words, in an information processing system, the users of the system can ask questions and get answers, as the need arises.

The main use of information is as the raw material for decision-making. It follows from this that two main features of an information system are: (1) a store of data which is large enough and correct enough to give valid and realistic answers, and (2) a system of linking each data item with any circumstances to which it is relevant. Clearly, if a man asks a question, he does not know the facts which provide the answer; moreover, he will probably not know about many or most of the facts which are or might be relevant to the answer.

Moreover, it is clear that 'units of information' are not necessarily crisply defined sets of letters or numbers neatly arranged in data fields. What about, for example, the information on which a judge decides a verdict, a scientist formulates a hypothesis, or a marketing manager embarks on a policy of opportunity marketing? How could such apparently vague and 'high-level' concepts become input data to a computer? The answer lies in a combination of human and computer efforts.

Why Computers are Needed for Information Processing

There is nothing the computer can do which is logically impossible for people to do. However, the combination of economy, speed and reliability is turning increasingly in favour of the computer; and yet again, one can do with a computer things one would never even attempt to do without one. This is particularly true with information processing. There are no intuitive or procedural short cuts bypassing the logic and the large amount of processing which information systems require.

How, for example, can the scientist hope, without a computer to help him, to retrieve virtually all the material which may be relevant to his work from the 50,000 different technical journals that are published throughout the world, each with its many articles?

There are certain clear reasons why the computer is used for this work:

The computer can organise, store and examine a vast amount of information at high speeds

It can undertake jobs of a scale that would otherwise be daunting, procedurally and administratively

It can come back with an answer and print it out very quickly

It can collect information (data) from remote sources and disseminate information equally remotely

It might appear that information systems could often be developed easily out of existing computer systems. For example, it might seem that a management information system should develop out of a sales accounting system, or a library information service out of a bibliographic system. The greater part of the source data is common to both; it can also be argued that a major step has been taken in channelling all the transactions through the computer system instead of through the sales accounting office. Moreover, a management information system can be developed on a fixed-report basis, using the same input data as the accounting system uses. For example, as well as posting an invoice to an account, the system may enter it into a planned set of reports, ranging between the detailed sales analysis and the profit and loss report. This apparent continuity is, however, deceptive. The existing data files, which may be on tape or designed as for tape even if discs are available, may be quite inadequate and unsuitable for the new task, both in content and in structure.

Even if it is feasible to ask the machine questions, it may be so uneconomic and time consuming that the users acquire no experience of using the information stored within their computer system.

An information processing system which will provide answers to users' questions must include the following elements:

1. It must accept a question which has been formalised according to the system's rules

2. It must identify and extract from within the system all data relevant to the request: 'information retrieval'

3. It must process the retrieved data in order to produce specific answers to the questions asked

4. It must present the answers

The first two of these steps in the process are the essential elements of information processing, while the second two are conventional data processing functions.

The first implies a language in which questions can be asked and programmed in the simplest possible way. Like all computer languages, this one will consist of a set of allowed words and rules for using them. It will contain a set of instruction words — 'list', 'total', 'equal to . . .' — which are common to many information systems, and a set of words belonging to the subject which is covered by the information system. The many fundamental issues raised by the linguistic requirements will be discussed below.

The second of our elements calls for mechanisms for data organisation and retrieval within the computer. These will include:

Mechanisms for putting new data into the machine and organising it

Mechanisms for recognising data items as being information relevant to a given request

Mechanisms for retrieving these items from the place where they are stored in the computer

Suitable equipment, with random access storage because one cannot predict where the next piece of information you will require is going to be

Procedures outside the computer to ensure the consistency and correctness of the information fed into the system

At this point it is necessary to describe briefly certain of the features which distinguish different types of information processing systems. These are:

The randomness of arrival of requests

The time allowed to the system for producing the answer

The number of records in the system's information bank that might have to be accessed to provide the answer

Two cases which are quite opposite in respect of these features might be: (a) a library system, in which users' requests require access only to several books out of hundreds of thousands, where the request is processed more or less at once and where the enquiry pattern is completely random, and (b) a business management information system, in which managers' requests may require access to a large proportion of the records stored. In the latter case, the question 'What were the total sales of brand X in year Y?' might need access to records of all customers who had bought brand X. A two-hour response time, say, is adequate; and in turn this means that requests which arrive randomly can be queued up and arranged in a sequence which suits the computer so that the retrieval process is made much quicker.

In the first of these cases, the computer cannot afford to spend up to, say, an hour and a half scanning all its stored information to get only several books. Complex indices and other information retrieval mechanisms direct it to the several records required; moreover, it is clear that all the information must be stored on 'random access' equipment which is 'on-line', for example, discs or drums (not magnetic tape).

In the second of these cases, the one which concerns us, the computer is going in any case to be looking at a reasonable proportion of the records. It is simpler and cheaper, for the computer, to take the queue of questions, to scan through the whole file at two-hourly intervals and to test each record in the file in turn for relevance to the questions. Clearly, immediate turn round and production of such reports in business is desirable, but it is in general—at the moment—impracticable or excessively expensive.

How Information is Stored and Organised in a Computer: Coding

The introductory remarks referred to the idea of a 'framework' within which data items become information. Clearly the individual data items must be linked into such a framework in order to direct one to relevant facts stored in the machine. For example, a library may have a book which is needed by a researcher because it is relevant to his work. This book must be linked with the framework of knowledge within which the researcher is working. These inter-relationships are defined through the process of coding.

The obvious main point of coding is to represent data efficiently within the machine; the point of indexing is to avoid having to look for a data item by searching through every record in the system. These in practice interact with each other and provide the basis of efficient information retrieval. Broadly speaking, data items are coded and then listed by indices (within the machine) which show where the associated information can be found—in just the same way as the index to a book directs one to a particular page. For example, a library book on the subject of Burgundian-Romanesque architecture may have index entries for each of 'Romanesque', 'Burgundian' and 'architecture'. Each of these entries will tell the program where, in the computer, to find the details of this book as well as of any other book on the same subject.

But coding does more than merely 'translate' a word or number into a set of computer hieroglyphics; while the main function of coding is to 'represent' items efficiently, it is powerful in that the code name for an item can show where that item fits into the scheme of things. Suppose we have a straightforward list of 50 names. We can give these the code numbers 1—50. Specification of the number 29 tells nothing about the name which '29' represents.

Suppose we have a large piece of machinery with many thousands of parts and many sub-assemblies. If we merely number each part, we have a long list of meaningless and unchangeable numbers. But if we break the machine down into sub-assemblies (*motor, gear box, control equipment* etc.) and each of these into sub-sub-assemblies (*motor*-shaft, *motor*-bearings, *motor*-stator . . .; *controls*-hydraulic motor, *controls*-hydraulic cylinder, *controls*-numerical control equipment . . .) and so on, we will arrive at a family-tree-like diagram with 'machine' at the top, sub-assemblies—motor, gear box, control . . .—in the next row, sub-sub-assemblies below these and all the unit components, wires, nuts and bolts etc., spread out at the bottom. Each unit or independent assembly can now be given a standard length part-number of which the first two digits represent the machine, the second two represent the sub-assembly and the third two represent the sub-sub-assembly. The part

number thus pins down exactly where in the machine the part is used
and what level of sub-assembly it is (gear box or screw). With such
a hierarchical coding system, detailed information about the inventory
requirements, parts' breakdown and bill of materials can be computed
with no need to make out a separate list of all individual items. This
would be particularly useful in, for example, a multi-product factory
using many components common to many of the products—'What is
the effect on inventory requirements of halving production of X and
doubling production of Y?'

While a hierarchical system can be extended to find room for virtually
anything, it cannot be used alone as the 'indicator of relevance' in an
information retrieval system. For one thing, it is far too precise. It is
very difficult to ensure that codes get allocated correctly; the person
hoping to find such-and-such a piece of information must specify the
same code number as was allocated to it when it was first fed into
the system. Close knowledge is necessary of the way things have been
coded.

If, therefore, the facts that make up the information stored in the
computer are coded in a hierarchical (or other) way, the user can always
find out exactly what to ask for—and what ground the system does
or doesn't cover. Indices are then called on to help the machine 'home'
quickly on any information in the system which is relevant to the user's
question—unless it is going to scan all the records.

How the Computer Finds and Retrieves Information: Indexing

The main technique in information retrieval for finding relevant data
is called co-ordinate indexing; this can be used in conjunction with
hierarchical codes. This method does not provide a unique entry or
pigeon-hole for every combination of subject matters; instead, it lists
the subject matters separately and describes each of the main data items
to which it refers.

The contents of the information stored in the computer are then divided
into two separate parts. The first part contains the descriptive properties
or 'subject matters' of the records, which we will call 'descriptors' (e.g.
the pay scale, department etc. of an employee; the region, account type
etc. of a customer). The second part contains the main data records
(e.g. the employee's name and personal data; the customer's name and
address, identity etc.).

In addition to the hierarchical and co-ordinate indexing techniques,
there is a third approach to the problem of retrieval which can combine
these two but which is logically independent of both. This approach
is known as 'chaining'—a technique by which each record or part of
a record refers individually to the next record with which it is logically

linked. Thus, all invoices to a given account might be chained to each other and to the account. Each record may be linked to several such chains.

So we have several basic techniques for finding things quickly within the computer, each of which can be applied to many problems in as many different ways. For example, in an advanced system it would take about $1\frac{1}{2}$ hours to read through about 5000 million characters' worth of data (perhaps one year's volume of sales data in a medium to large firm); whereas given our co-ordinate indexing system, it could take less than half a second to retrieve a relevant data item. The time taken to execute a search and to answer a question depends on many issues. A simple question involving the retrieval of a single record can be answered in a few tenths of a second, plus the time taken to ask the question and print an answer. A question which is more complex, either in the sense of the complexity of its logic or in the sense of the number of records involved, can become a major processing job occupying many minutes on a large computer.

Asking the System Questions

Although we might like to ask the computer questions such as 'tell me the profitability and growth rate of . . .', we cannot, unfortunately, speak into the computer down a voice tube—at least not now or in the immediate future! The question must be turned into the language of the computer system, being made entirely specific in the process. Thus, terms like 'profitability' will have to be defined in terms of the data already within the machine—selling prices on invoices, costs of materials, labour, services etc.

In fact, as soon as one starts asking how a user expresses himself to the system, or how ideas and information are formulated before being presented to the system, the various linguistic aspects of information retrieval and processing must be considered. Just as there is a whole range of types of information processing, so there is a wide range of questioning techniques. These range between, on one hand, having the use of a short and pre-defined list of words for phrasing requests, and on the other hand, studies on the contribution to meaning made by words, sets of words and syntax, so that users can communicate with the system in free language, relying on the system to assess the relevance of stored information to their questions.

The words in which a user frames his request to the system can accordingly be separated into two categories: 'information words' and 'command words'. The 'information words' identify items of information, e.g. sales, brand prices, discounts, rates data, census data etc.; and the 'command words' represent the instructions telling the system what to do with the items of information, e.g. print, add, total, equal to, list, excluding etc. The following example of a command to a report generator (question and answer) system will show the difference. Command words are in italics and all other words are either 'information words' or ignored:

List sales (of) products *in* product groups A, B, X, Z, *between* 1.1.74 *and* 1.9.75 *showing totals by* product, outlet type (and) territory, *excluding* sales (of) products to jointly owned outlets, *for each quarter. Suppress totals less than* £500. *Print summary total on change of* territory *and* product group.

This is the kind of request that needs a fairly advanced report generator system. The balance between the information words and command words varies between types of systems. For example, at the simple end of the scale, a library information retrieval system may require the user to code his requests so that he only actually feeds in information words; the arrangement of these on the form he fills in or the terminal he is using represents the commands to the system. At the other end of the scale is the highly selective research worker selecting very specific information.

A case where the emphasis is heavily on the use of command words is a finished goods stock control system which is 'controlled by exception'. The computer can be provided with forward-order information, carry out forecasting on the basis of past sales, and can then compare both with the finished goods stock position. The same instructions can apply to a whole range of goods, and only the cases where the forecast and the short- or medium-term position depart by more than a given amount from the forecast are listed for the management.

These 'linguistic' issues should not be confused with the computer languages such as Cobol, Fortran or Algol. The programs which interpret the user-requests to an information system may be written wholly or partially in one of these computer languages; but the linguistic facilities made available by information processing systems are aimed at non-computer experts—librarians, military strategists, medical researchers, town planners, and business managers. These linguistic facilities are the product of an attempt to go as far as is technically and economically feasible towards enabling these people to use the language and terminology they know. It is essential to make these systems simple if they are to become both used and useful.

Efficiency of an Information Retrieval System

The efficiency of such an information retrieval system is very hard to measure, because the decision as to whether something is relevant to a given situation or problem is subjective; and because one rarely has the opportunity to find out everything that the retrieval system has missed.

The normal measures of efficiency are 'relevance' and 'recall'. 'Relevance' is the percentage of retrieved items that are relevant. 'Recall' is the percentage of the relevant items held in the system which are retrieved. These terms have the interesting property of being mutually conflicting—the higher the recall, the lower the relevance, and vice-versa. This is intuitively clear if one realises that a system which retrieves everything that might be relevant (i.e. high recall) is bound to produce a lot that is irrelevant (i.e. low relevance). If on the other hand one eliminates everything that might be irrelevant, one is bound to miss things that are relevant.

PLANNING AND CONTROL SYSTEMS

We will now look at the third class of systems. We have seen that transaction systems process movements of money or materials and that information processing systems provide a means of answering managements' questions. Planning and control systems do some of the managers' routine work. By drawing on the information about transactions, and by following a policy statement rigorously when alternative decisions are open to it, a computer can 'decide' how much of a particular material to order, or which supplier to order it from, or how much to make next month or whether to supply customer X who hasn't settled his account. The computer takes no decision of course, but if management lays down the rules, and then modifies these rules as circumstances change, the computer will carry them out. It is really becoming quite useful when it does this, because it will carry out the rules consistently and accurately, without fear or favour and with regard to much more information than a human controller could handle.

The use of the computer in this way, helping management to control and allocate money, materials and people, will be fully discussed in the second part of this book. Here, in this chapter on systems, we will look at the sort of rules management has to lay down for planning and control systems, taking stock control as a typical and widely relevant example.

Raw Materials Stock Control

Stocks are held to provide a service—to provide goods for sale on demand, to feed a production unit or to keep vital buildings and equipment in working order. Inadequate stocks have an immediate and powerful influence on manufacturing efficiency and customer satisfaction. Excessive stocks give good service but are generally a most wasteful way of tying up working capital.

Lack of balance, with some items in short supply (inevitably the vital ones) and others held in large quantities, gives the worst of both worlds.

Unfortunately this situation almost always prevails to some extent, imposing a heavy burden on management.

A computer can help to ease this burden both by reviewing all stocks frequently and by enabling alternative policies to be tested rapidly and painlessly before implementation. The computer system will follow a set of basic rules laid down by management, and assistance with this can be obtained from many textbooks. For each group of similar items, depending upon value, delivery time, relative importance to the business etc. the safety stock, delivery quantity and level of service (i.e. how often stock can be allowed to run out) will be determined. The level of service is of fundamental importance and a good stock control system should be able to react quickly to a single management decision to 'cut the level of service by 25%'.

The delivery quantity should maintain continuity of supply between successive deliveries, the safety stock is kept to cover the demand if delivery is delayed. When the safety stock falls to zero it is providing its maximum protection. A computer can assist management to ensure that this happens in a predicted, controlled way and, for example, only on fast-moving vitally important items.

The delivery quantity can be constantly reviewed by a computer and even where simple control systems are used such review will usually more than repay the effort involved. There is a natural tendency to order quantities which are too large for real needs, particularly for an item where the demand rate is declining. Manual systems are slow to scale down the delivery quantities, consequently the delivery interval lengthens and the average stock level fails to fall as it should. A computer's value comes from its ability to monitor continuously and to make comprehensive changes when commercial conditions change or when budgets are being prepared and it is desired to estimate inventory values for various levels of activity.

The approach to setting up a computer-based inventory control system starts with three sets of decisions:

1. The level of service required from each item (or group of items)

2. The rules to be used for determining order quantities

3. The total value of stocks which the business is able to support

These are not independent decisions and the first two may have to be modified to satisfy the third.

The control system itself may be of a simple type, called 're-order point control', or it may be more sophisticated. We will briefly look at a 'schedule control' system, one of the latter type, after considering re-order point control.

In a re-order point control system the stock of an item is allowed to be consumed without action being taken until the quantity of available stock falls to, or below, a pre-set level known as the re-order point. A fresh supply is then ordered. If the re-order point were set correctly (one can know this only in retrospect), the existing stock would be exhausted just as the new supply became available. If the re-order point were too high, there would still be stock on hand when the new supply was delivered and stock in excess of the ideal would be carried. If the re-order point were too low, a 'stock-out' would occur before the new supply became available.

The time from the signalling of the need for fresh supplies until the new supplies are available in the stores is the replenishment delivery, or lead, time. This period is in the future at the time of the decision to order fresh supplies. The calculation of the re-order point must, therefore, start with a forecast of future demand. In practice it is also necessary that this forecast be revised frequently so that the control system follows drifts and other variations in the level of the demand for the item.

Traditional systems of stock control mostly fail in this respect—the re-order point is not revised frequently enough. The more sophisticated methods of demand forecasting which have been developed in recent years are easily handled by a computer, but are beyond the capabilities of manual and simple mechanised systems of control (unless the inventory is comprised of only a few hundred items) because of the sheer volume of calculations that may be called for.

Various methods of forecasting the demand for items may be used. Moving averages is the simplest one, and it is as well to stick to this method (remember, simple things *work*) where the value of the stock items requires nothing more complicated. More sophisticated forecasting methods are available—exponential smoothing gives more weight to the most recent demand data; Box-Jenkins smooths out the variations in demand and is good where large variations upset the forecast. Seasonal variations in demand upset any forecasting system unless allowance is made for them. A simple forecasting system *which management fully understands* is undoubtedly the best. No system will deal with all eventualities so a monitoring system is used in addition. Regularly, the monitoring system analyses the forecasting errors for each item and signals when the system is failing to respond quickly enough to a real change in demand. Management may then intervene and if they consider that the change will be sustained, the sensitivity of the forecasting system may be temporarily increased until the system has adjusted to the new level of demand. In the simplest system the sensitivity is increased by taking the moving average over a shorter period of time.

The optimum delivery quantity for each item is a function of such factors as:

1. The cost of placing the order, chasing it, accepting delivery, updating stock records etc.

2. The demand

3. The cost price of the stock item

4. The cost of holding the item in stock, valuing it periodically, deterioration etc.

5. Quantity discounts available

A standard work should be consulted for information on the implications of these factors. The purpose of mentioning them here is to give management some idea of the level of detail they need to go to if they want the best from a computerised control system.

Earlier we mentioned schedule control. This is relevant where stock items are expensive, where demand tends to vary significantly and where demand is determined in advance by management decision. Schedule control bases stocks on future rather than past performance. A system which is integrated with production will base stocks upon the production plans which have been laid down by management. The computer is particularly useful for estimating the cost of stock to service various production plans and can break this cost down month by month for the duration of the production schedule. This information is then available for budgeting cash resources in the same way that factory resources and labour resources may be planned.

Finished Goods Stock Control

Much of what has already been said about raw materials stock control applies equally to finished goods. However here the time taken to produce a stock unit or batch of units and the production batch size are to be used instead of the delivery time and delivery quantity. Re-order point control is used for finished goods stocks, but where firm customers' orders are placed in advance of delivery very great savings in stocks may be made.

Pre-posting of demand is always to be preferred when it is possible for the computer to have access to the customer orders before they go to the warehouse. Details of each day's orders would be passed to the computer in batches. Those customers who are to receive preferential treatment with items in short supply would be indicated by means of a priority code.

Details of the requirements would be posted to the stock record and a note made of any item which could not be supplied immediately. If the stock were inadequate to cover all demands in the batch of orders, the available stock would be allocated in accordance with the priority code. The invoices may then be prepared with the non-available quantity of each item annotated 'to follow' and omitted from the price extensions. The non-available items would also be omitted from the warehouse picking lists and packing notes. A credit control routine would suppress invoices or parts of invoices which exceed the customer's credit limit and arrange to cancel the stock allocations affected.

As part of the processing of each item, the revised balance of available stock would be checked against the re-order point and a list printed of new replacement orders required. Alternatively, or in addition, information on replenishment orders could be recorded on, say, magnetic tape for the subsequent automatic preparation of the orders themselves. Stock receipts would be posted to the stock record at the same time as, or before, the new requirements are posted. Details of any outstanding, unfilled sales orders would be examined and invoices and packing notes printed automatically for the items now available.

A daily total of the value of stores issued and received and the opening and closing stock balances would also be produced for each stock group so that management may have a daily report on the inventory. This report could include the value of customer orders not met (shortages) and of outstanding replenishment orders and show how values have changed during the day.

In cases where the customers' orders are serviced by the warehouse before details are passed to the computer—for example, where branch warehouses deal directly with customers and report later to a central computer on what they have supplied—there is no question of allocation. In all other respects the system could be the same if the invoices are to be prepared centrally. If suitable data transmission links were used between the branch warehouses and the computer, it would still be possible to operate a stock allocation system as already described.

Stores Auditing

In all inventory control systems the accuracy of the recorded stock balances used by a computer-based system is vital to efficient control. The computer may always be relied upon to check its own working and no undetected errors will come from that scource. Clerical errors in the data fed to the machine are still possible and these cannot always be checked by the computer. Errors in computing receipts and issues may also occur as can losses in breaking bulk, in storage (evaporation) and in pilferage.

In these circumstances an annual stock check will almost certainly be inadequate and it will usually be necessary to operate a system of continuous inventory checking. Moreover the likely risk of error needs to be determined for each class of stores item and the frequency of checking set to suit.

Since the records are now contained on magnetic tape or direct-access storage devices, it is best that the computer determines which items shall be checked each day. Given the desired frequency of checking each item, it can be instructed to generate random numbers which achieve this frequency and it can issue daily lists of items to be checked without anyone being able to predict the contents of any list. At the same time it would prepare a record of the current stock balance and recent transactions of each item selected so that the stores' auditors may verify the checkers' count against the recorded balance. Stock may not be checked at the time relative to which the computer calculates its balances. The stores' auditors must make allowances for this.

MANAGER OF INFORMATION

We have now looked generally at all three classes of computer system, and discussed the more difficult concepts in some detail. The management team which wishes to add a computer to its number must be aware of the implications of saying 'let's put stocks on the computer' and the same goes for any other system, be it transaction, information or control. We hope this chapter has thrown light on those implications.

Just suppose an applicant for a management job told you that in addition to the job you had described to him, he had a photographic memory and would be able to remember:

1. All the orders placed by customers
2. All the materials ordered by your company
3. All the production resources
4. All the customers' accounts
5. All the available staff and operatives, what they can do and what they are costing you
6. All the stocks of materials and finished goods

Not only that, he says, but also he can analyse all these facts so that if you specify a sales forecast, he will tell you whether you have the production resources and raw materials to do it. If you specify a production plan he can tell you what raw materials you will need to order, and when. If you specify a maximum cash flow he will tell you how best to spend it. Further, he will carry out simple rules and exercise a measure of control over orders, stocks, production, credit and anything else where you can define the rules of the game. I think you would take such an applicant into your management team. Your computer is applying for the job.

CHAPTER 3

Other Uses the Manager Can Make of his Computer

By J. R. Birkle

In Chapter 2 we considered the three types of commercial systems which constitute the day-to-day work of a computer which is trying to earn its place as part of the management team. These systems, it will be remembered, were concerned with processing transactions, with controlling everyday occurrences such as stock movements and with analysing and printing statistics.

As a part of the management team the computer must not be so inflexible as to do this and nothing else. It has an abundance of 'brain-power' which, provided it is directed towards problems within its capability, can be used to assist other managers who from time to time have a variety of one-off problems to solve. The word 'assist' was very significant there. No computer can take decisions on other than the simplest of day-to-day questions without human help because the world is not a tidy, logical and static place in which everything is either black or white.

The problems faced by management can of course be answered one way or another without the use of a computer. There is rarely a right and a wrong answer; it is a matter of assessing all the relevant factors—or as many as can be measured—weighting them according to one's judgement of their importance, quantifying their effect on the problem in hand and then reaching a decision.

There are three reasons why a computer can sometimes improve a manager's performance in a decision-making process, and more than one of these may apply to any particular problem. The three occasions when it is sensible to ask the computer to give some help are when:

1. There are too many factors for the manager's brain to consider simultaneously

2. The calculations involved in quantifying the effect of the factors are too numerous or too lengthy or too difficult for the manager's mathematical ability

3. The amount of operating experience available in the situation is so slight that the effect that changes in the factors have on the outcome

cannot be measured directly. However, if the relative effects can be predicted and the inter-relationships defined so that a model of the problem can be set up (in mathematical terms) then the computer's speed can be used to concertina the time-scale and to test the predicted effect of a variety of planning assumptions

There is a fourth class of problem with which the manager may need help. This is where a decision must be reached, but the information that is available and relevant is not sufficient to enable a solution to be based on fact at all. Unfortunately the majority of decisions fall into this class and the manager must take care to recognise them. For if they pass unrecognised into the computer's hands that well-meaning machine is likely to produce an 'answer' based on the partial and in-sufficient data it has been given. The computer's answer tends to receive far more credence than it deserves and quite erroneous conclusions may result. It cannot be stressed too strongly how much of the skill in using a computer for problem-solving lies in knowing when *not* to use it, and, when it *is* used, knowing how much importance to give to the computer's solution.

For the remainder of this chapter we shall look more closely at the three classes of problem that lend themselves to computer-assisted solutions. The intention is to illustrate the way in which a computer can assist managers—not to provide a textbook on how to use these techniques. A manager wishing to apply his computer to problem-solving should study one of the many books on operational research techniques.

To illustrate the computer's role where the facts are too numerous we will examine critical path network processing. Then in a mathematical role we will look at 'linear programming' and 'queueing theory', and in a modelling role we will briefly consider the movement of goods by road transport.

NETWORK PROCESSING

The aim of critical path network processing is to break down a complex project into very small constituent parts so that these become individually quantifiable and controllable. Such projects as constructing a motorway, a ship or a building are obvious candidates but rather outside the experience of most managers. Introducing a new product or moving an office or factory from one site to another is more likely to be of general relevance. Any project involving many people and materials, which needs to be completed in the shortest possible time, and with minimum use of resources, can be considered for this approach of reducing it to small and manageable operations. These operations are defined in terms of events and activities.

An *Event* is a point in time that can be identified with the achievement of some discrete aim, usually the termination of some element of work which is part of the project. An *Activity* is an element of work, or the passage of time that is required to pass from one event to another.

In drawing a network it is usual to represent an event by a circle, identified by a number, and to represent an activity by an arrow pointing from one event to another, thus:

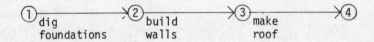

dig
foundations
build
walls
make
roof

Not all activities are sequential like this. In some cases many activities may start simultaneously as soon as an 'event' has taken place and in others an activity may start soon after the start of another activity, but not simultaneously with it. There are techniques of representing such activities on a network. Some activities may not use any labour or material resources, but just take time (which is a most important resource). Such activities as drying concrete, or waiting for plans to arrive in the post come in this category. Another obvious contingency is that some apparently unconnected activities may depend on one man, or one piece of equipment and therefore cannot be undertaken simultaneously.

Bearing all this in mind, or at least trying to, the network planner represents the logical sequence and interdependence of activities on a very large piece of paper: Having done this he considers the effects of time. The first stage is to select the units—usually days, but any other unit will do, so long as it is maintained throughout the network.

The next step is to give each activity a duration. This is the estimated time that it will take to perform the activity with the resources available. It may be advisable to work with the 'worst case' and 'best case' estimates as well as with the 'most likely' estimate to see what the total effect is.

Having allocated a duration to each activity it is possible to calculate the earliest start and finish times for each activity. In a similar way, by looking at the finishing date for the project as a whole, the latest start and finish dates for each activity, such that they do not hold up the whole project, can be calculated. Any do-it-yourself man who knows that through his own efforts he has to buy materials and find time to do a variety of jobs must mentally run through this process which we have described. Almost instinctively he tackles his planning, his buying and his handywork in a sensible sequence so that he doesn't have to sit around with time to spare, unable to proceed because the shops are closed or his neighbour has borrowed his power tool. Magnified a hundred-fold the problem is still soluble by a careful planner with plenty of time. Much larger than this and a computer becomes useful because of the accuracy and speed with which it can handle all the detailed calculations.

Somewhere in the network there is a sequence of activities linking the start and the earliest finishing date such that any activity taking longer than its estimated time will delay the completion of the project by that additional time. This particular sequence of activities is called the critical path, and the activities on it require particularly careful monitoring, all other activities having a certain amount of slack time or 'float' available. During the lifetime of the project, if slippage on the critical path occurs, other paths may become critical as a result of resources being transferred to activities on the previous critical path. This may be far from obvious by inspection and lengthy to calculate by hand. The use of a computer to analyse the network can highlight such occurrences very quickly. An inexperienced planner, using a computer, can avoid making the mistake of worsening a situation he is trying to improve.

Summarising the advantages of using a computer for helping the planning function in this way:

1. The results are accurate and illogicalities are removed

2. The documentation is produced automatically

3. It is easy to amend the network as resources change and estimated times are exceeded or improved upon

4. The computer can sort and reorganise this data, extracting work schedules in any desired sequence or format

CONTROL OF RESOURCES AND COSTS

So far we have looked at the help the computer can give in controlling the time taken to complete a project and in reducing the time taken in replanning a project. Three other resources, closely related, must be controlled—people, equipment and costs.

Most of the activities will have a certain amount of 'float' or spare time associated with them. It is human nature to start all activities as early as possible in order to retain as much time in hand as possible. However it is not necessary to start everything as early as possible and in fact it is undesirable to do so. It leads to premature investment of capital, idle time for labour and equipment and unnecessary peaks in resource utilisation.

A network, carefully drawn and fully analysed for time constraints as described above, can be re-analysed to smooth the requirements for resources. Again this is quite possible to perform by hand, but the frequency with which it must be revised, and the simple repetitive nature of the calculations, make a computer the obvious choice once the number of activities exceeds 300 or so, or the number of resources more than 1 or 2.

The computer program will be able to optimise the use of a resource, for example, men or machines, in order to limit the number required at any one time or to limit the total consumption of a resource, for example money, during the life of a project.

By using the 'float' on each sequence of activities not on the critical path, the program will schedule the activities according to the availability of resources. Some management constraints will usually be present. These take the form of:

1. Dates that impose restraints on the schedule. Examples are: required completion dates, resource availability dates and required commencement dates

2. Restrictions on the way the program may handle activities. These may be to ensure that certain activities are carried out consecutively, or are not split in execution

By changing the management constraints, particularly the completion date, dramatic changes in the resource requirements are sometimes produced. It is usually worth experimenting with this just to see the effect. The network is really a model of the project on which various tests can be carried out. This modelling capability of the computer will be mentioned later in this chapter.

When a resource scheduling program is scheduling activities, it is trying to fit them into the framework erected by the availability of resources and of time. If it does not have sufficient resources, it will delay the activity until the resources become available. If it has no time to play with, it will try to re-schedule other activities. It is likely to reach a point where it can satisfy neither requirement. The manager using the computer has to step in then and decide which is more important, time or resources, so that the program can proceed with some course of action, although second best. Some programs provide for 'threshold' resources that are more expensive than normal ones. This can reflect the use of overtime or hired men or equipment. Sooner or later, though, it will come back for the decision which only management can take: what are the relative consequences of using more time or more resources.

Network analysis provides a flexible tool for planning purposes. However, the achievement of its effective use lies outside the manipulation of activities, events, resources, and decision tables. It is vital to ensure that the network is drawn at the correct level for those who are going to use the results. To take an extreme example, it is no use presenting a managing director with the schedule for dismantling and cleaning an oil storage installation that gives the details of each tank to be opened and the processes to be performed. A common error is to make networks too detailed. In drawing a network, one must consider the following factors:

1. The responsibilities of the users of the schedules
2. The prime requirements of the project in terms of time control and use of resources. It is not necessary to schedule the use of each nut and bolt in the assembly of a ship
3. The fact that it is impossible to reflect in detail all the complexities of modern industrial life
4. There must remain sufficient flexibility for those in immediate contact with the project to modify schedules to take into account such imponderables as changes in the weather, machine breakdowns, and labour absenteeism

The technique is best used when the project requires the integration of the activities of different departments or companies. In many cases, where an activity can be reduced to the responsibility of one department, then it is best to leave it at that, so that the department concerned can control its minute to minute performance. For example 'make tools' is usually the responsibility of the tool room. It is usually best to leave the tool room manager to implement the activity. He may find it valuable to use a network for his own department, but this should not be incorporated in the main network.

USING THE NETWORK

The plans of all projects change as they are implemented, and one of the major advantages of network analysis is the ease with which plans can be changed. For example, a contractor constructing a major road improvement scheme may find that the actual soil structure through which a cutting is to be made is different from that expected from the soil samples taken. This actual structure may require plant not immediately available on the site. If the project was initially planned by network analysis, and processed by computer program, the affected parts of the network would be redrawn, and hence new completion dates calculated together with work schedules and resource requirements, within 24 hours of the decision to replan. The power that the computer makes available to the planner is the ability to foresee quickly the effects of events that cause a major change in plans.

These events can be from natural causes, such as the example of the contractor, or such events as labour disputes or even changes in specification of the project controlled. Research and development projects, where progress from certain events depends on the results of certain activities, can benefit particularly well from the ability to replan and re-assess the whole situation quickly and accurately. A useful facility provided by the computer is the ability to allocate responsibility codes to each activity, and then to use these codes to make the computer print out schedules for each manager or department responsible for particular functions.

The progress of a project must be reported back to the network to ensure correct implementation. Most computer programs allow the ability to report progress, and then re-schedule the network. The frequency of updating must be selected with care, as too frequent updating causes confusion and too infrequent updating does not give enough control. The frequency must therefore be selected to suit:

1. The users of the results

2. The nature of the projects

It is best to integrate the network with the cost reporting system, so that a statement of costs and performance against time is presented to the management concerned.

Although a true picture of the project's development in relation to time can only be obtained by reporting the progress of each activity, it has been found that to attempt to report costs against each activity creates confusion by the large number of cost centres defined by the network in the shape of the activities. However, it is very effective to group activities into cost centres and to report costs against these groups. Some computer programs have facilities to achieve this grouping and reporting, and the system will therefore provide reports showing the relationship of the project to cost and time.

THE COMPUTER AS A MATHEMATICAL TOOL

We will now turn to the second class of problems where the computer's mathematical ability makes it a useful tool. Management spends a great deal of time both in predicting the likely outcome of future events and in balancing available resources against conflicting demands. Many of these problems may be expressed in mathematical terms and exact solutions obtained instead of the inspired guesses of the past. The advent of the operations research department in industry has meant better solutions to bigger problems and the computer is the tool which enables the large amount of mathematical work that is often involved to be done in a reasonable time scale.

Although this section is essentially a discussion of the application of mathematics rather than the underlying theory, some reference to theory is first necessary in order to define and limit the field of discussion—this is particularly desirable in view of the nature of the subject.

Mathematics is a conceptual framework which can assist in the study of the real world, but which never describes the real world precisely; it is an abstract, man-made framework which can be studied as a self-contained system and can be made self-consistent. Herein lies its power. The complexity of real life (including business problems) can be simplified and brought to 'manageable proportions' from which patterns of structure can be determined. It is these patterns in which we are particularly interested, since only by study of patterns can we predict what might happen in the future—a disordered collection of facts tells us only what has happened and this with not much understanding. The true solution of a business problem, or at least that class of business problem to be considered here, is obtained only when one can predict the outcome of future actions with a known degree of confidence. This conceptual framework can therefore be considered as a system more amenable to study than the real situation to which it approximates, but to which it approximates closely enough for the results to be of practical use.

The mathematical framework contains methods by which the degree of approximation can be rigorously defined and quantified, so that assessment of the reliability of solutions is not left entirely to subjective judgement. This is the field of statistics which for this purpose can be considered as a bridge between the abstract mathematics and the practical business world.

The point to be remembered is that the mathematical models that are built and the solutions that are obtained will be idealised ones, some of which will closely describe the real thing, whilst others will be rough approximations. All of them however, used with sound judgement, will be better than the pure guesswork that is very often used to solve commercial problems.

The field of mathematics in business is very large. What part of this field are we to discuss? What kind of business problem? What kind of mathematics? What examples are illustrative of the principles and also easy to comprehend from a brief description? We are concerned with operational problems of strategy, of reconciling conflicting aims—the area of management decision-making. The mathematics will be characterised by the methods of solution in that a precise answer can be obtained by analysis or numerical methods, or that the solution can be reached by a systematic and converging process. The meaning of 'converging process' will be made clear in the text.

One final point before we begin to discuss applications—why do computers come into all this?

Many of the solutions can be obtained only by numerical or converging methods; a series of repetitive calculations is employed, each successive calculation getting nearer to the answer because the mathematics is so designed and is not a trial and error process. The number of calculations is often very great, too great to undertake manually—either too lengthy or too costly. There are also mathematical models which are too complex for practical analysis, even though the method of approach can be determined and it can be proved that a solution does exist: there are too many variables to manipulate at one time. The computer is ideally suited to dealing with both these situations because it can perform calculations at immense speeds and handle a large number of variables at one time. Calculations which, manually, might take many months (and thus be of no value in dynamic business situations) can be condensed to a few minutes in computer time. In this context, one must distinguish between this process of condensing the time taken to perform the calculations, and that to be described later in the chapter where the time scale of actual business operations is condensed by simulation on the computer. Here the computer is used primarily as a tool of mathematics, although in application the mathematics may not be evident—the manager communicating in very simple terms with the computer.

The first field of application that we will discuss, and one which highlights this particular use of the computer, is linear programming. This is a technique which broadly can be described as a means of allocating competing or alternative resources (or supplies) to meet conflicting demands in order to optimise the 'return' from the system. The resources may be production processes, chemical raw materials (supplying constituents of manufactured chemicals), rolls of paper (supplying smaller rolls), job applicants (supplying the skills for particular jobs), warehouses (supplying goods to a number of depots), garages (supplying vehicles to pick-up points), foods (supplying vitamins for a diet) etc. The returns to be optimised might be costs to minimise, profits to maximise, job efficiency to maximise—i.e. the objectives of the solution. The term 'linear' is used because the costs, profits, efficiency measures etc. are directly proportional to the number of units considered and at the same time the number of units supplied are directly proportional to the number of units of input; in other words, the mathematical relationships thus formed to represent the system could also represent equations of straight lines on a graph. We can illustrate here how mathematics begins in the solving of these problems: the above description of linear programming is fairly lengthy, not very precise and not very amenable to analysis. The mathematical statement is as follows:

Find values of x_{ij} where $(i = 1, \ldots, m; j = 1, \ldots, n)$ which optimise (minimise or maximise) the linear form

$$\sum_{j=1}^{j=n} \sum_{i=1}^{i=m} c_{ij}x_{ij} \qquad (1)$$

subject to the conditions

$$x_{ij} \geq 0 \tag{2}$$

and

$$\sum_{j=1}^{j=n} a_{ij}x_{ij} \leq b_i \quad i = 1, \ldots, m \tag{3}$$

where the a_{ij}, b_i and c_{ij} are constants determining the supply and demand restrictions and costs, respectively.

Although this appears rather forbidding to the layman and tempts him to replace the book on the shelf, there is really nothing much to it. It is merely a convenient shorthand notation.

Σ means 'the sum of all the factors following', and the suffixes 'i' and 'j' merely indicate general values of the different variables or constants considered. The 'm' and 'n' show how many different values of the suffixes must be included in the summation and thus, how many different variables. If you consider the variables in a grid it is easier to understand (*see* diagram).

x_{11}	x_{12}	x_{13}	. . .	x_{1j}	. . .	. . .	. . .	x_{1n}
x_{21}	x_{22}	x_{23}	. . .	x_{2j}	. . .	. . .	. . .	x_{2n}
x_{31}	x_{32}	x_{33}	. . .	x_{3j}	. . .	. . .	. . .	x_{3n}
.	.	.		.				.
x_{i1}	x_{i2}	x_{i3}	. . .	x_{ij}	. . .	. . .	. . .	x_{in}
.	.	.		.				.
x_{m1}	x_{m2}	x_{m3}	. . .	x_{mj}	. . .	. . .	. . .	x_{mn}

Each 'x' with its suffixes represents a different variable. These variables are then set out in ascending order of the suffixes, the first suffix representing a label for the row and the second suffix representing a label for the column in which the variable is to be placed. These 'labels' would also correspond to the sources of supply and the points of demand, respectively. Thus x_{23} would represent the amount to be sent from supply point number 2 to demand point number 3. So that we do not have to write down every variable, we show the first few variables in each row and column to indicate the sequence of the suffixes and then use 'i' and 'j' to indicate a generalised position in the table, just as we use 'x' to indicate a general variable. x_{ij} is a typical element in the table, 'i' representing its row position and 'j' its column position; the 'm' and 'n' are used to indicate the maximum number of rows and columns in the table and thus the last row will be labelled 'm' and the last column will be labelled 'n'. This means that we should have exactly 'm' supply points and 'n' demand points.

We can thus indicate a large number of equations very concisely and also provide a means of stating a problem in general terms, so that we can manipulate it without constantly having to remember whether we are talking about vitamins or transport fleets. One of the major difficulties of application, however, is to realise that these general equations fit one's own particular operational problem, and to choose suitable units in which to express the requirements and resources; the ability to do this is largely dependent on the skill of the operations research man, but fortunately there are now many tried and tested examples which can be used as bench marks to compare with one's own problem. Additionally, the computer industry gives a comprehensive service in this field by providing 'packaged programs' for a large range of linear programming applications. There are two major benefits in this: the applications can be easily recognised with the required data being specified and, secondly, the costs of solution are very much less than if one had to undertake the initial research and program writing.

A SIMPLIFIED PROBLEM—TRANSPORTATION

With these programs one need not know anything about the underlying methods of solution, but in order to illustrate the place of mathematics in all this, we shall solve a simplified problem by manual methods. The example we shall take is solved by the 'transportation technique' whose origins will be fairly obvious; it is a restricted technique in that it can be applied only to those problems where the requirements and resources can be expressed in one kind of unit, but it is easier to follow than the more general techniques. In mathematical terms it means that the a_{ij} of equations (3) are all equal to unity.

Suppose that there are three motor agents who require delivery of 5, 7 and 6 identical models, respectively. The main distributor has three depots from which he can supply the cars, and he has in stock 4, 6 and 8 cars respectively at each of the depots. The distances from each depot to each agent are different; therefore, at a fixed cost per mile, the distributor's delivery costs will depend on how he allocates the cars to the agents and he will wish to minimise these costs. The delivery costs per car (rate x distance) are shown in Figure 3.1.

AGENTS DEPOTS	A1	A2	A3
D1	£3	£4	£6
D2	£4	£3	£5
D3	£2	£4	£2

Figure 3.1

The inequalities involved in the problem are as follows:

$$x_{11} + x_{12} + x_{13} \leqslant 4$$ (4)
$$x_{21} + x_{22} + x_{23} \leqslant 6$$ supply restrictions   (5)
$$x_{31} + x_{32} + x_{33} \leqslant 8$$ (6)

$$x_{11} + x_{21} + x_{31} = 5$$ (7)
$$x_{12} + x_{22} + x_{32} = 7$$ demand restrictions   (8)
$$x_{13} + x_{23} + x_{33} = 6$$ (9)

where x_{12} represents the number of cars being supplied from depot 1 to agent 2 etc.

The total delivery cost will be:

$$c = 3x_{11} + 4x_{12} + 6x_{13} + 4x_{21} + 3x_{22} + 5x_{23} + 2x_{31} + 4x_{32} + 2x_{33} \qquad (10)$$

and this has to be minimised. We can put all these constraints into one table (*see* Figure 3.2).

AGENTS DEPOTS	A1	A2	A3	SUPPLIES
D1	④ £3	£4	£6	4
D2	① £4	⑤ £3	£5	6
D3	£2	② £4	⑥ £2	8
DEMANDS	5	7	6	18

Figure 3.2

Our first task is to find a feasible solution (not necessarily the optimum one) which is consistent with the supply and demand restrictions and this we have done already in Figure 3.2. The numbers are circled. This is how we did it:

Start with the 'northwest' square.

Compare the demand for that column (5 cars) with the amount available from that depot (4).

Allocate as much as possible to this square (this will be the least of the two values).

If demand exceeds supply (for that square) move to the next square vertically and repeat the process with the outstanding amounts. If the converse, move horizontally and do the same. If demand equals supply move diagonally. In this way, all the restrictions are satisfied and you will note that columns and rows total correctly. Also, the number of squares filled (5) is one less than the number of supply points plus the number of demand points. This is a mathematical restriction related to the independence of the initial data. The cost of our first solution is:

$$c = 4 \times 3 + 1 \times 4 + 5 \times 3 + 2 \times 4 + 6 \times 2 = £51.$$

We now start to converge from our feasible solution to the minimum cost solution.

For any square that we have just filled, split the actual costs into two 'fictitious' costs, say of despatch and acceptance.

$$C_i + C_j = C_{ij}$$

The two fictitious costs on the left of the above equation are arbitrary and for the first square it is convenient to make one of them zero, thus fixing the other one. We then work round the other four filled squares in a similar way, so that all the arbitrary costs are consistent (*see* Figure 3.3).

DEPOTS \ AGENTS	A1 £3	A2 £2	A3 £0	SUPPLIES
D1 £0	④ £3	£4	£6	4
D2 £1	① ← £4	⑤ ↑ £3	£5	6
D3 £2	↓ £3 ——→ £2	② £4	⑥ £2	8
DEMANDS	5	7	6	18

Figure 3.3

With the aid of the arbitrary costs we now examine if any of the four unoccupied squares could be utilised to advantage and to do this we compare fictitious costs with actual costs, for each of these squares.

If the actual costs are less than the two fictitious costs (which were determined from the present solution) then we ought to utilise that particular square.

In this particular case the use of square D_3A_1 would give a lower cost (and it happens to be the only square). In D_3A_1, the actual cost is £2 and the fictitious cost £2 + £3 = £5.

We therefore move as many cars as possible into square D_3A_1. (If there had been more than one unoccupied square with a cost saving potential we should have chosen the one with the greater potential.)

In order to keep within the initial constraints the rows and columns must still balance and so if we add to any square we must subtract from another square in the same row and from one in the same column. This takes us in a closed circuit round the table as shown by the arrows. Since we must keep the same number of occupied cells and since we cannot subtract more than is already there, the circuit must consist of occupied cells (other than the initial cell) and we can only transfer the smallest of the values in the chosen circuit.

It is '1' in this case, from D_2A_1. Figure 3.4 shows the new table.

AGENTS DEPOTS	A1	A2	A3	SUPPLIES
D1	④ £3	£4	£6	4
D2	£4	⑥ £3	£5	6
D3	① £2	① £4	⑥ £2	8
DEMANDS	5	7	6	18

Figure 3.4

The new cost is:

$$c = 4 \times 3 + 6 \times 3 + 1 \times 2 + 1 \times 4 + 6 \times 2 = £48$$

which is lower than the first solution.

We then split the costs again and repeat the same kind of calculations until we find that all the actual costs are less than or equal to the current set of fictitious costs.

For this example we have in fact reached a minimum solution, as you can test by putting in your own fictitious costs.

The least cost for this set of deliveries is therefore £48.

A practical situation could involve far more variables than we have used above and one would have to repeat the calculations many times. This is an ideal problem for the computer to take over and it makes an overlengthy academic exercise into a viable commercial proposition.

GRAPHICAL PRESENTATION

Now you ask 'Why does the above set of calculations produce an optimum solution?' This can be answered by showing the geometrical representation of the problem.

The equations represent straight lines on a graph and so we shall draw these lines. Since we can draw only in two dimensions we shall have to take fewer variables than before so let us formulate a new problem:

Suppose a retailer had a contract to spend at least £21 per week with his supplier of grades A and B of a certain chemical, and that these items cost £3 per ton and £7 per ton respectively. The retailer has 10 cubic yards of storage space available and can get deliveries only once a week; item A occupies 2 cubic yards per ton and item B occupies 1 cubic yard per ton. The current accepted retail prices of A and B are £6 and £11 per ton respectively and the market is unsaturated i.e. the retailer can sell all his capacity. He wishes to maximise his profits. This is represented by the following equations:

$$3x_1 + 7x_2 \geqslant 21 \qquad (11)$$
$$2x_1 + x_2 \leqslant 10 \qquad (12)$$
$$x_1 \geqslant 0, \quad x_2 \geqslant 0 \qquad (13)$$
$$P = 3x_1 + 4x_2 \qquad (14)$$

x_1 and x_2 represent the amounts in tons of A and B;

Equation (11) represents the contract with the supplier;

Equation (12) represents the storage restrictions;

Equation (13) means that we cannot have negative weights;

Equation (14) represents the total profit, P, the coefficients showing the profit per ton (Figure 3.5).

All points to the right of $3x_1+7x_2=21$ satisfy the corresponding in-equality (11) and similarly, all points to the left of $2x_1+x_2=10$ satisfy the inequality (12) together with $x_1, x_2 \geqslant 0$. Therefore, the combined solution must lie in the shaded area. Our calculations are a means of shifting

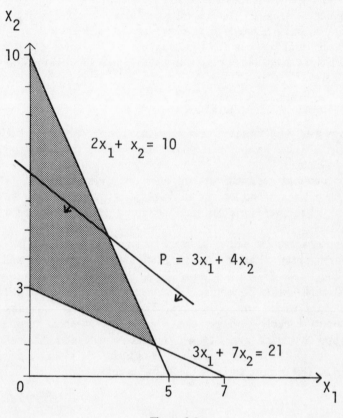

Figure 3.5

the profit line until it reaches its minimum distance from the origin, within the shaded area. By inspection this would be the point (0, 3). The analogy can be extended to more than two dimensions, but the problem could not of course be solved by inspection as above.

EXTENDING THE SCOPE OF LINEAR PROGRAMMING

Because of the variety of units involved, this last problem could not be solved by the same computational methods, the transportation technique, as our original car problem, but would involve what is known as the simplex technique. Belying its name, it is a more complicated procedure than that we have described, but is applicable to a wider class of linear programming problems where the requirements and resources can be expressed in different kinds of units. This aspect is reflected in the coefficients of the variables in the constraint equations, which in the transportation problem were all unity, but for the simplex process need not be so. These coefficients represent the relative contribution to the final requirements made by each of the resources associated with the corresponding variable. To make this clearer, we can refer to equations (11) to (14).

In equation (11) the coefficients '3' and '7' represent the contribution to cost that x_1 tons of A and x_2 tons of B would make.

In equation (12) the coefficients '2' and '1' represent the contribution to volume that the same weights of A and B would make.

In equation (14) the coefficients '3' and '4' represent the contribution to profits of x_1 tons of A and x_2 tons of B i.e. (£6–£3) and (£11–£7).

You can see the different units with which we are involved—weights, volumes, costs and profits.

This problem is of course trivial in that the solution is obvious from inspection and no simplex calculation is necessary, but in practice one would be dealing with more variables and this would give rise to greater complexity. Since the simplex method is fairly lengthy and is well covered by available literature, we do not intend to go into details here, but merely to stress the need for computer facilities—for practical purposes one could say that a computer is essential since the number of combinations and permutations increases rapidly for even moderate numbers of resources and demands. Even with a high speed computer the solution of some problems of linear programming is prohibitive by the methods mentioned above and short-cut methods have had to be developed.

We have dwelt at some length on these techniques because they are particularly suitable for demonstrating the relationship of mathematics to business problems and highlighting the way in which computers make a practical business proposition out of mathematical theory. They are not the only linear programming systems. Many others have been devised, sometimes to reduce the vast amount of computation and in other cases to take account of special restrictions. Vehicle scheduling is one example, where one is attempting to find the least costly means of allocating delivery routes to a number of vehicles. The simplex process is too lengthy for day-to-day use and it is not necessary since the problem can be formulated in such a way that the x's are restricted to two values, one or zero. If a vehicle is to take a particular branch of a route, the 'x' is one; if not, the 'x' is zero.

PROBLEMS OF CONGESTION—QUEUEING THEORY

The next class of problem that we wish to discuss is that of queueing theory, again a field of well-developed techniques, but where the use of computers will not be so evident. Nevertheless, there are situations in which the mathematical analysis is practicable only by a computer and others where constantly changing data needs continual processing, a task not very efficiently undertaken manually.

Queueing problems arise when a service facility is subjected to varying demands at varying frequencies. The service facility might be a super-market cash desk with customers arriving at different intervals of time and each checking-in a different number of goods; the performance of the cashier will also vary. Even though on average the cashier is quicker to check out the goods than the customers are in collecting them, there will be some occasions when a customer with a short order arrives behind one with a long order. If the second customer has to wait too long she may not patronise the shop again. Conversely if there are too many idle cashiers ready to speed customers through, overheads will be too high and profits will fall. The problem is to determine the minimum number of cash desks that will keep customers happy. The same kind of problem arises at petrol stations, in factories, where one process is serving others, on roadways serving traffic, in restaurants which have to provide sufficient but not too many tables and waiters, at telephone exchanges where the number of lines must be balanced with the number of calls and in a host of similar situations.

The queue is due to the variation in service and demand times; if the times were fixed we could arrive at an exact balance so that one 'customer' departed just as the next one arrived. The mathematician is mainly concerned with those queues that are controllable, where the average demand is less than or equal to the average service facility; if the converse were true the queue would continue to grow indefinitely and the situation would be out of control. In some cases this does happen for short periods of time, e.g. when an accident occurs on the roads, and the usual solution is just to wait.

One method of approach to these problems is first to determine the patterns of service, arrival and levels of demand by means of probability formulae, and then to list the probabilities of the system changing one state to another in a small period of time, e.g. one customer arriving whilst another is still there, one customer departing before another arrives etc. The total probability of there being a certain number in the queue at a particular point in time is then the sum of the individual probabilities of reaching that state. Equations are thus built up to show how the probabilities change with time and the equations are then solved to indicate the changes of there being 1, 2, 3, ... etc. in the queue at *any* time.

This in turn shows how long customers might have to wait under different levels of service, thus enabling the manager to fix an appropriate level. These equations are known as differential equations, and the easiest situation to solve is that where the system is in a 'steady state' i.e. although there may be fluctuations, the service just keeps pace with demand, sometimes getting ahead, sometimes dropping behind.

There are other forms of solution which use different kinds of equations, but all involve the aspect of variation which can be expressed only by statistical methods. This means that there will be uncertainty in the answers, but the statistical methods will also be capable of assessing the reliability of results and will show probable patterns of events, from which policy can be decided.

Many queueing situations are exceedingly complex due to a multiple combination of different service channels and demands and unusual patterns of distribution of the various time factors involved. Computers are an extremely powerful tool in these situations. They can generate these non-standard probability equations or distributions from original data and can then be used to investigate the whole range of possible combinations to predict the behaviour patterns of the complete system. Further, they are able to produce numerical solutions in situations that defy an analytical approach and where the basic factors of data are rapidly changing. Not least is their capability of printing control information for these rapidly changing situations such as industrial manufacturing processes and air traffic problems, for the bare mathematical 'solutions' are not generally in a form readily usable by the operating manager.

At the end of this chapter queueing problems are discussed which can only be solved at present by simulation techniques as opposed to the analytical approach discussed here.

MACHINE INTERFERENCE

One final point on queueing theory—there is a special class of queueing which has wide application in manufacturing industries. This is the field of machine interference which occurs in the operation of semi-automatic machines. By semi-automatic we mean those machines which will run without intervention for short periods of time, but which then stop and need to be replenished with materials and restarted. With one operation, one machine, the cycle is the sum of the running time, plus replenishment time. If, however, you allocate more than one machine to one man, a machine may stop whilst he is attending to another and there is thus an additional delay or 'down-time' for the second machine, which in turn will happen to all the machines in that man's care. The output of three machines, say, is therefore not necessarily three times that of one machine. In general, the less machines a man has, the more he will be idle; the more machines he has, the more machine down-time will occur. It is management's job to balance these two factors. This is a closed queueing system where the machines are customers returning cyclically for service. A number of solutions to this problem have been obtained which show expected levels of idle time for various numbers of machines and various cycle times. For continually varying production programmes and fluctuations of the labour force, the results need constant and quick modification if full efficiency is to be maintained. Computers again provide an ideal facility where these calculations can be integrated with production control routines.

REPLACEMENT OF EQUIPMENT

The problems of machine operation lead us to a further class of business problems amenable to mathematical analysis, that of equipment replacement. Machines (and other equipment) wear out; maintenance costs begin to increase whilst new equipment needs capital. Initially, the maintenance and depreciation of equipment cost less than interest lost on new capital expenditure, but at some point in time there will be a change-over, a break-even point. The problem is to forecast when this point will arrive and to plan the replacement of equipment accordingly. Here again we are faced with uncertainty; the rate of decay of equipment will vary, interest rates will change and the discounted value of future costs must be determined. Replacement theory is a set of techniques devised to handle these kinds of problems. The mathematics is often quite complex since it has to deal with many different conflicting factors at one time, with the effects of the performance of one item on another, with different 'generations' of equipment and with financial priorities. Also, in addition to equipment which deteriorates, there is equipment which fails suddenly and this may have disastrous effects on other activities. At the same time, one does not want to replace needlessly and this calls for sophisticated statistical techniques. As with some queueing problems, the generation of statistical patterns and the manipulation of them would be impracticable without the use of a computer. The mathematical models would be too simple and idealised and the degree of uncertainty would be unacceptable. The computer can thus bring the level of uncertainty within acceptable limits and give us a workable solution.

MODELLING

Finally we will look at the third class of problems in which the computer can be useful. The technique can be generally described as modelling or as simulation. A model of a situation which needs studying is set up (in numerical terms) within the computer, and this model is made to respond as nearly as possible in the same way as the real-life situation. Then by using the speed of the computer to try, try and try again, the model can be used to indicate in a very short time what might happen to the real-life situation over a period of weeks, months or years. The effect of changes on the model (the bank rate, inflation, the number of men or machines available, the number of orders received etc.) can then be tested individually or in combination until eventually a decision can be taken on the situation under study.

In addition to regular events which management can predict, the real world is full of irregular happenings which disrupt the best laid plans. These can be introduced into the model, without knowing precisely what causes them or what their effect will be, by constructing a frequency distribution based on past experience or hunch. During the simulation process a pattern of disruptive events is then produced by the computer at random times. Over a sufficiently long run of the model this procedure will reproduce the average effect of the random factor. The joint effect of several random factors can similarly be represented by introducing several different sampling distributions into the model. Situations often regarded as not capable of quantitative treatment, due to the presence of irregular factors, can thus be analysed.

VEHICLE SCHEDULES

Problems closely related to those discussed above arise in connection with the operation of a fleet of transport vehicles. Management often has to take into account the influence of many complex and somewhat unpredictable factors on the demands for, and the proposed movements of, vehicles. The basic problem here arises from the fact that the number of vehicles in the transport fleet is fixed, but demands vary from place to place and from time to time in a complex and often unpredictable way. It is thus not always possible to plan in advance to supply vehicles immediately to the points where they are required. Also mechanical breakdowns, bad weather or other unforeseen factors can reduce the number of available vehicles to below that planned, in which case scheduled services will be held up unless standby vehicles can be called on without delay. The problem is complicated by the fact that delays at one point are likely to cause 'reactionary' delays at other points, especially if movements are planned in advance to a tight schedule with few built-in buffer periods for catching-up time, and if connections between services have to be maintained so that passengers or freight can be transferred between vehicles or handling machines. One primary delay may then spark off a whole chain of consequential delays and disruptions at other points in the transport system.

In view of the above it can be seen that some of the decisions facing managements when planning new services, installations or schedules depend on the correct evaluation of some exceedingly complex factors. Some questions demand very careful analysis, for instance: how many vehicles should be provided in order to ensure an adequate standard of service for users, or to provide smooth and rapid cargo handling with minimum of unusable waiting time? Should standby vehicles be provided, and if so on what occasions should they be used? When is it economic to make positioning movements with empty vehicles in order to avoid delays or cancellations to services? What services should be cancelled or combined, rather than delayed?

A simulation model provides an excellent means of studying such questions and avoiding costly mistakes in the design of new systems by enabling their consequences to be viewed in advance. The simulation technique has hence been widely used in this context, particularly by airline planners when designing new time tables (aircraft movements are particularly vulnerable to disrupting influences), suppliers of lifts for tall buildings where fluctuating and unpredictable demand conditions have to be serviced on different floors, and production managers in steel works and other manufacturing plants wishing to know how many gantry cranes, trollies, trucks and other items of handling equipment they need to support a given level of production activity.

Models may be made of any dynamic situation—of stock levels at various points in a production process, of customers' ordering patterns, of the cash flow of a company, of the British economy etc. As a technique for the manager facing up to a problem it is not of much use unless the model has been built and tested previously for this may take several months. However, once prepared it may be modified and used again and again.

This chapter concludes our look at the computer and the way it is generally applied to management problems. In the remaining chapters we shall consider specific ways in which the management may use the computer, and the information it produces, to improve the efficiency and profitability of a commercial enterprise.

CHAPTER 4

The Control of the Flow of Money

BY R. S. D. STINTON

In this chapter we are to deal with the way in which computer-based systems can assist in the 'control of the *flow* of money'. It is intended to concentrate upon financial accounting as opposed to management accounting which can be defined here as the control of the *use* of money.

It is intended to deal with cash flow under two broad headings:

1. *Cash receipts,* that is all aspects of the way in which computerised system support can assist the control of receivables. The primary objectives are to collect *all* the outstanding debts quickly and to minimise 'costs of collection' commensurate with the annual amount of bad debts to be written off against profits

2. *Cash payments,* for example, salaries, invoices. The primary cash flow objective is to make outgoing payments at the optimum time

Whilst it is easier to be more specific about particular types of applications concerning receipts and payments, it should be clearly understood that the attributes of these two aspects of the control of the flow of money need to be married to the overall, external cash flow management policy laid down by and monitored by the company's financial controller e.g. liquidity changes as affected by stock, debtors, cash at bank, creditors. The subject of cash management policies is dealt with in greater detail in Chapter 5.

The way in which the cash flow computer system can be developed with a capability of marrying together the total company situation will depend upon the local answers to the three main classical aspects of feasibility of any large computer system.

1. Operational feasibility. Taking the long-term view, can everyone be satisfied that a totally integrated system is capable of being properly staffed and used? Will adequate facilities be available to meet the company's changing needs? The final decision on these matters can only be taken by the users of the proposed computer systems.

2. Technical feasibility.   Are the data processing professional advisers employed on designing the system able to assure the user managers that an effective combination of hardware and software can be assembled? Are the mainframe equipment, data transmission facilities etc. available from reputable manufacturers in the present and future capable of supporting the type of system envisaged?

3. Economic feasibility.   Do the future marketing prospects of the company or group appear to warrant the establishment of a partially or fully integrated system? Alternatively, should the different aspects, e.g. debtors' control, be designed and developed separately with the subsequent option to consider further development or integration at some point in the future? Is it possible to identify sufficient cost savings and benefits which will adequately justify the proposed investment in the system?

It is to be stressed that any comprehensive system designed to support the financial accounting area should inter-relate to the overall company business objectives wherever possible. Where this is difficult, caution should be exercised. A staged approach should be adopted, albeit that the subsequent integration of stages may require a certain amount of re-design and re-programming. More is said on this subject in the later section dealing with flexibility of systems.

I have attempted, in the next few paragraphs, to consider separately the ways in which computer support can be given to receivables, outgoings and cash flow in general. In the section at the end of this chapter, where the problems of file structure are dealt with, I have attempted to summarise the advantages and disadvantages of designing a fully integrated system.

It may already be well appreciated, but I must nevertheless stress again, the paramount importance of the total involvement, commitment and contribution of senior user management to the work of designing, approving and implementing the systems discussed. They must be fully involved at every key decision stage.

CASH RECEIPTS

SYSTEMS FOR SETTING UP THE DEBT

After marketing and sales have done their job and the goods are delivered or services rendered, the information becomes available to the account handling/debtor control system to enable the debtor's account first to be created (initial transaction) and then increased (additional sales). Wherever possible this information should be a by-product of the systems already set up for carrying out the work/providing the services: job ticket, stock accounting, delivery notes etc.

An important point to recognise is that the efficiency of the interface between the various systems—computer and non-computer—is as important as the actual systems themselves.

Operational Feasibility/Costs of Data Gathering

It is important to decide at an early stage in planning the strategy for data gathering. At a determined point in the system, the input data will need to be converted into machine readable form.

One of the decisions needed will concern centralisation or decentralisation of the data preparation section. To give a simple example of designing a system to provide data for a centralised computing unit, there are two choices:

1. Transmit in paper form, e.g. invoices, the information to the central office. There the appropriate choice of input machine would be engaged upon converting the data into machine readable form to be then passed into the computer system. The original paperwork would be centrally available to answer any input queries but would probably be then passed back to the point of origin. Employing this method would concentrate the data processing expertise and achieve the economies of scale

2. Recently there has been a very rapid increase in the use of terminal devices. Taking a sophisticated example, it is possible to equip remote locations with television-type terminals with a typewriter keyboard capable of converting data into machine readable form. The mode of communication between these remote terminals and the central computer unit can vary. At a cost there can be a continuous Post Office wire link which will enable a considerable amount of data checking to be carried out by the central computer to highlight any input errors. Alternatively, the remote terminals may operate off-line using the appropriate amount of 'local intelligence' capable of doing some checking, totalling etc. Periodically, e.g. daily, the locally stored information can be transferred to the central unit over a Post Office wire or perhaps in the form of a magnetic tape transported to the central office. It should be mentioned that some of the types of terminals available for data input are also capable, where they are connected with the central computer by telephone line, of accessing the debtors' master files.

It is important to consider thoroughly the consequences of the method chosen for data gathering. There are indeed a very large number of alternatives and special variations. Once again the need to preserve the maximum degree of flexibility is important. In those circumstances where the new system to be created is a significant advance upon the old, there could well be merits in using the simplest of methods in the early stages and developing more sophisticated techniques in the subsequent years.

Invoicing

In the ultimate, the production of invoices is merely a job of 'printing'. With modern computer equipment, this job can be done in any location. The detail of the information which is to be printed upon the invoice will be drawn from the master computer files maintained for the general debtors' control, stock control etc. In an increasing number of instances, these file maintenance and manipulation activities may well be centralised with good advantage.

Credit Vetting

During the stages prior to carrying out the work or delivering the goods etc. the information stored on the debtors' control system might well be interrogated to determine whether the company has had dealings with its prospective customer at any time in the past. If information has been recorded, then this might be used to ensure that the appropriate 'credit terms' are again offered to the customer.

In the consumer finance market e.g. where the repayment of a debt is to be spread over a number of years, it is obviously advisable to establish the prospective customer's credit worthiness. A number of alternative computer systems can be of assistance, for example:

1. If the customer has had previous transactions with your company, then the computer can make reference to the previous accounts and ascertain the type of debtor status built up

2. From the information required to set up the customer's record within the computer system, it will be possible to extrapolate on a points rating basis, the customer's credit worthiness. Such a system would be in the nature of a supplementary guide to the salesman whose opinion might well over-rule the assessment made by the computer.

Recording of Debts

Given that there is a need for accurate systems design and programming, a debtors' control system, once it has been fully tested, provides the best way of securely controlling account details. Information stored on either tape or disc files and subjected to well-defined control standards within, say, the computer system, provides the financial accountant with a much higher degree of reliability than he can expect from conventional ledger card systems. In addition to the security benefits, there is also the added advantage of increased confidentiality.

Debtors' File—Design of Content

The opportunity should be given to all sections of the company to participate in this aspect of the design of the system. Bearing in mind the costs involved in creating and maintaining files, care must be taken to ensure that no area is neglected. If it is subsequently found that large parts of necessary information have been omitted, this would jeopardise the effectiveness of the system. Depending upon the time scale within which the omissions were detected, it may take a disproportionate amount of cost to repair the damage and virtually reconstruct the file. It is therefore advisable to make the job of defining and approving the details to be stored on the file one of the first tasks to be undertaken. On pages 76–8 details are given of an example file structure/content with comments upon indexing systems.

In cases where a computer system is being designed to take over from existing procedures, it will be well worthwhile to check carefully through the nature of the existing records to ensure that all necessary data is to be captured and stored.

UPDATING THE DEBTOR'S ACCOUNT

Having initially set up the debtor's account within the computer system, this file will need to be kept up to date with cash postings, file amendments etc.

Methods of Payment

A computer system affords an increased variety of methods of assisting customers to pay, such as:

1. Direct debit. Under the system now operated through the Bankers' Automated Clearing Services, a magnetic tape inter-change can be effected for the transfer of monies due e.g. on rating accounts. This system lends itself more suitably to the payment of regular, e.g. monthly, amounts and the authorised amounts are transferred within the precise terms set out within the authority given by the customer.

The particular advantage of magnetic tape inter-change of direct debit payments is the improvement to the time scale in bringing the money to the credit of the creditor company's bank account. In general terms the money is credited on day one; under other systems, e.g. counter payments or cheque payments, the money is not credited until days two, three or even four.

2. Turn around documents. The computer system facilitates the production of invoices including a tear-off, fully referenced payment slip, capable of passage through the Bankers' Automated Clearing Services, postal services etc.

A number of types of 'machine readable' methods of production are available e.g. the stub portion of the invoice can be produced readily from a computer high speed printer in a form which can be read by electro-mechanical means when it is returned together with the payment.

Promptness of Posting

As an essential ingredient to the control aspects, the availability of a computer system will enable the speedy processing of cash payments to be handled as a matter of routine. Where the system can be cost justified, each of its receipts is processed i.e. batched, totalled, corrected and applied to the master file on a daily basis. The state of the file after each nightly update is immediately available, both in total and in detail by separate accounts. This is particularly helpful at the close of an accounting period. The further, added advantage is the prompt availability of the up-to-date state of each account which can contribute significantly to the overall efficiency of the work of clerical supporting staff and also add materially to good customer relations. An up-to-date account reduces the amount of estimation in the preparation of arrears-letters, bad debts etc.

The work of producing reminder letters or undertaking legal action for collection of cash is confined to the appropriate circumstances. The ability to keep the file right up to date and thereby send reminders consistently and promptly when accounts fall into arrears significantly reduces the chances of non-payment. It is important to present invoices promptly and accurately. It is equally important, particularly in the consumer market, to take every prompt step possible to *prevent* arrears occurring i.e. produce whatever prompting reminders are possible to ensure that your company's invoice is paid in preference to others.

Accuracy of Postings

In any debt control system, it is vital to ensure that payments received are appropriated and posted to the proper account. It is possible to build into the computer system cross-checks which go a long way to prevent mis-postings. Most computer systems, by default, work on customer index reference numbers: all transactions concerning a customer's account will bear this pre-allocated number. The number may well incorporate a check digit. An alternative is to 'match' each payment not only on the reference number but also with the customer's name or a part of the customer's name.

Automatic Cash Reconciliation

The reconciliation of cash is defined for this purpose as the work involved in ensuring that: (i) all cash received is paid to the bank; (ii) all amounts banked are eventually posted to the appropriate debtor account.

The decision on whether or not to use the computer to assist with cash reconciliation will largely depend upon the degree of computerisation of the financial records. From the comments made above, it can be seen that computerisation of (i) the debtors' accounts and (ii) management information records might well be maintained by a suite of computer programs. It does not necessarily follow that the company's financial records and accounts are maintained on the computer. If the decision to computerise the financial activities can be justified of itself, it must follow that the ability to computerise/automate cash reconciliation will be possible. It is difficult to be precise in making a single recommendation. There are inevitably problems of different time scales e.g. 'the day's bankings' do not necessarily constitute one day's input to the debtors' control system. Problems of postal delays etc. mean that a flexible system of reconciliation must exist. Depending upon the number of accounts, the number of collection points, the different methods of receiving cash, the decision must be taken on the extent to which cash reconciliation is taken out of the hands of the clerical function.

It seems likely that the general movement towards the cashless society, even though the movement is so slow as to be not even visible, leads to the assumption that further computerisation will follow. In the case of the direct debiting system, a magnetic tape is already produced for payments/payments due. This tape is produced by the creditor company and is used by the Bankers' Automated Clearing Services to create the debit postings to their customers' bank accounts. Beyond the production and inter-change of tape, little work is left by way of reconciliation.

There is inevitably the problem of 'untraced accounts' i.e. payments received which cannot be readily identified with the appropriate debtor's account. A well computerised debtors' system should provide a ready access to accounts via enquiry terminals (see page 63). Wherever possible and economically justified, enquiries might be made of the debtors' master file by the use of a multiplicity of keywords e.g. part name, part address, reference number, merchandise code, amount of debt outstanding etc.

To conceive a system where the method of cash reconciliation is fully automated requires the existence of a highly sophisticated and totally integrated suite. If the company's business is such that such a level of computerisation is normal and to be expected, then within this range will be included the maintenance/production of financial accounts. Within this area will follow the job of cash reconciliation. Where this level of computerisation has not been reached or perhaps cannot be justified to the same extent then the reconciliation work might well have to be handled by manual methods. Once a proper system has been established the work is not too time consuming or costly and the fact that it is maintained clerically will provide a significant degree of flexibility.

In summary the question of reconciling bankings to postings can only be justified in the light of the degree of computer procedure integration. It would not be fair to say that such a job should never be automated.

COLLECTION OF OUTSTANDING DEBTS

Having created the file of debtors, established a system for applying cash payments and ensured that adequate file character and cash controls are in force, the system is ready to be put to use as a debtors' control tool.

Before considering the debtors' control system and its effect upon cash flow, it is worthwhile appreciating that the amount of effort and cost involved operationally in getting to the stage mentioned above might well account for some 70% of the computer system costs.

It is also useful to remind ourselves that the primary objectives are to collect all the outstanding debts quickly at the optimum cost.

Periodically the state of each debtor's record must be examined by computer program. This can be done on a cyclical basis e.g. every ten days. It is also worthwhile building into the system a check upon the state of the account each time a cash posting is applied. When designing the system of arrears follow-up, it is necessary to determine the extent to which the work of collecting arrears is to be carried out by computer program, e.g. automatic production of reminder letters, against that part of the work that needs to be done manually, e.g. taking legal action. This is an important step in the design considerations. It will have a large bearing upon costs, clerical staff and hardware requirements.

It is important to schedule the cycle of examination of account states to optimise the use of the equipment and provide a regular flow of work to non-computer sections.

Taking the case of a debtors' file comprising several hundred thousand records, then a reminder system might consist of the following stages:

a. Daily update including the addition of 'new debts' (sales), application of cash payments

b. Examination of the summary information stored in the leading part of each record showing the amount and age of debt outstanding following application of 'today's' payments

c. Production by computer of reminder letters for debts still outstanding beyond the period of credit laid down. Differing types of letters, i.e. differing in content and layout, would be produced according to the age and size of the debt and possibly taking account of the payment patterns stored for this customer regarding previous transactions. Letters could include notifications of intention to take legal action. Indeed there is no limitation on the information to be printed provided that the relevant supporting information has been gathered into the debtors' system

d. Production of listings of outstanding debts that have reached the stage where routine automatic action is not expected to be effective and where manual intervention is required. In the case of a public utility this might result in the arrears notifications being sent to district offices for calls to be made on the non-payers

e. Special accounts—where details were stored within the system denoting the existence of some special circumstances to be borne in mind when following up arrears, these would be recognised by the computer program and the appropriate notification produced and sent to the section dealing with 'special accounts'

f. Court action—where the next step was to take legal proceedings, the appropriate paperwork would be produced from the debtors' system

The above system gives no more than an outline. As many or as few local variations would be designed into the system according to the choice of user managers.

It should be borne in mind that the arrears notifications do not need always to be in paper form unless they are being sent to customers. As mentioned in a later section, information can be made available on microfilm /microfiche or via visual display terminals.

It is suggested that the state of a debtor's account is examined each time a posting is made. There can be many variations of states resulting from the application of payments. It is important to decide in the design stages, the extent to which the computer programs are intended to determine automatically the appropriate course of action to be taken e.g. where a discount is allowed for prompt payment, then the computer program can ensure that a payment within the laid down limits is accepted as full settlement and a further generated posting is created to ensure that the balance of the account is reduced to zero.

Through the medium of the computer control programs, it is possible to control and vary the periods of credit allowed for different regions, customer groups etc. It might be necessary to allow variations by season e.g. to recognise the special circumstances prevailing at Christmas time when customers' payments may be delayed in the post. The computer system should have sufficient flexibility to provide for these *ad hoc* variations.

Calculation of Accrued Interest

The work involved in the calculation and application of amounts of accrued interest e.g. on cases of arrears and non-payments can be the most time consuming clerical exercise. Under certain circumstances, where very large volumes of accounts are concerned and particularly where relatively small cash balances are involved, the work of calculating and collecting accrued interest may need to be cost justified. Given the support of a computerised debtors' control system, such a facility, once properly programmed, will cater for various accounts, large and small, and can readily amended to give discretionary relief e.g. by merchandise groups. Variations to the rate of interest to be charged can be made quite simply.

ACCESS TO UP-TO-DATE INFORMATION

One thing that any computer system can provide in plenty is information. In the area of debtor control, the information can be made readily available both for internal and external purposes in a variety of ways.

Paper Copy

Information can be produced in any form, layout or printing style. Where necessary the paper output can be produced in a form ready to be mechanically handled and enveloped for postal distribution.

Simplification of Presentation

It is possible, at no extra cost, to simplify the presentation of information. The information printed on invoices and statements can be set out with maximum clarity and, if it is thought to be of benefit, the style of the invoice etc. can be personalised by the use of upper and lower case printing.

Visual Display Terminals

Information stored in a computer's data bank can easily be made available in locations, both central and remote. On a simply operated television-type terminal by the entry through a keyboard of the appropriate index, it is possible to obtain the details of the whole or a part of a debtor's record. Such access can be made in a matter of seconds. There is no subsequent filing away of paper. The next time that the display is required, it is readily available and indeed would then reflect the most recently updated state of the account. It is quite feasible to employ the use of a slow speed printer, also located alongside the visual display terminal, which can be used to provide a copy of selected accounts or part accounts. Alternatively the visual image can be captured by the use of a polaroid camera.

Microfilm / Microfiche

Any information already stored within the system can be extracted in the form of microfilm /fiche. Such a storage medium has a cost /space advantage over paper. Where information is required to be passed to remote locations, postage costs are considerably reduced. At the location of use, it is necessary to have the appropriate reading equipment.

MANAGEMENT INFORMATION

Given that the required information is stored within the computer system, i.e. the original data recorded at the time when the account record was set up, plus (a) transaction data for postings made and (b) history data of reminders produced /sent and also letters produced then, from the information stored, a multiplicity of management reports can be extracted. Indeed, caution must be exercised before fresh reports are designed and introduced which simply add to the mounting pile of paper that the computer system can so easily provide. It is recommended that such management information reports are invariably (a) produced on an exceptions basis, limiting the amount of information preferably to comparisons of actual against planned figures, or (b) produced on request only i.e. not at regular fixed intervals. The information may be categorised:

1. Control details by clerical section, geographical area with analyses and totals of new debt, cash postings
2. Arrears: amount and age of arrears, percentages against total debt outstanding
3. Bad debts: analysed with projections on prospective bad debts based upon historical payment /non-payment patterns stored on file

The use of information retrieval packages avoids the need to develop and digest routine monthly or weekly sets of reports. It is well worthwhile considering the rent or purchase of a packaged program which will extract and present information according to variable parameters specified by user managers.

FLEXIBILITY

It has always been strongly stressed that the user manager should think most carefully and deeply about *all* of his present, medium- and long-term requirements. Even in the best regulated circles there seems to arise the need for a phase two! However carefully thought out the initial systems concepts are, there will subsequently be changes to: the law, taxation, markets, products, management, accounting practice and auditors' needs. Any one or combination of these factors will probably necessitate change and on-going change.

Management should avoid wherever possible the development of a gargantuan system which, although it may be thoroughly reliable and stolid, will inevitably prove difficult and costly to maintain.

As stated above, maintenance will be required and, unfortunately, cannot be avoided. The only circumstances in which on-going maintenance will not be needed is if you are planning to go out of business.

It is stressed that flexibility is a *must*. Every attempt should be made to employ a 'modular approach' to both thinking and designing. I feel that the overall benefits to be gained from the adoption of a flexible and modular approach outweigh the possible advantages of producing a more sophisticated system which might, in its compacted form, require less computer running time and capacity. This principle clearly applies to many general aspects of computer systems design and is not a point which is especially applicable to 'debtors control'.

MEASURES OF EFFICIENCY

Payment patterns vary from year to year and from region to region. It has been recently stated that 'debtor morality' has declined. Non-paying customers are no longer unduly concerned at the prospect of door-to-door collection or even the threat of legal proceedings. As stated previously a manager may be satisfied that his debtor control/debt collection system is thoroughly *efficient*. However, because of the change of circumstances, its *effectiveness* may have become impaired. By using the capabilities of a computer system it will be possible to monitor performance, to vary the recovery action employed in different areas as mentioned above, and to attempt in a more scientific manner to maintain the most effective system bearing in mind all external factors.

Measuring Efficiency

The relative functions performed both by computer program and within the adjacent clerical control and data preparation area should be closely examined. The costs of current systems employed can be analysed in detail because the introduction of a computer system, particularly one of a sophisticated nature, will have required the detailed investigation of all of the steps involved in the calculation and application of receivables and all other aspects of cash flow.

After specification of the computer system there exist a set of procedures and a deployment of resources that more readily lend themselves to an outside investigation of cost effectiveness. The unit costs incurred in collecting monies by varying methods can be compared e.g. direct debiting method compared to postal remittances. Here again is a further aspect of the way in which a computerised system offers a greater opportunity for tighter cost control.

Monitoring Changes to the Collection System

Even though the system in force may be thought to be efficient it may be difficult to quantify its effectiveness, particularly in its primary objective which is the control of bad debts. With a computer system it is easier to make partial modifications e.g. for a geographical area, and to monitor the effect of the changes. At any one time it would be possible to run a number of controlled experiments in order to determine the most effective system for a class of customer, type of business etc.

CENTRALISATION

The merits of centralisation versus decentralisation pose an age-old problem for any company. Such problems as there are can be further aggravated by the inter-company divisions that one finds perhaps within a group or conglomerate organisation. It is often said that the running of the data processing department matches those problems of organising a company i.e. combining the problems of planning, funding and production scheduling. It is therefore obvious that the same problems are met with when attempting to determine what is the balance of advantage i.e. whether one should centralise or decentralise the computer function. It is perhaps more truthful to talk of the computer functions because there are different considerations relating to central processing and to the location of input and output activities. Some of the general organisational problems which are met with across the broad spectrum of company affairs are to a degree less complicated in the data processing field because of the flexibility provided by the ease and speed of modern data communication and transmission techniques.

The facility of a computer system to provide immediate access to up-to-date information can also provide a most useful opportunity to decentralise some of the operations. It is not necessary to centralise the activity responsible for answering enquiries. Where there is a balance of advantage to provide information retrieval facilities to decentralised locations which are also sales outlets and which have a regular local contact with customers then the computer retrieval facilities offer a wide range of choice.

The centralisation of processing using the computer mainframe provides the opportunity to take advantage of the economies of scale of equipment, with the concentration of development expertise. It must be borne in mind that there are inherent problems in having all one's eggs in one basket i.e. adequate security arrangements and back-up facilities must be maintained.

The centralisation of the derivation and production of debtor information in the form of the periodic invoices and also statements will necessitate the establishment of the facilities needed to input raw data concerning sales etc. Sales outlets will be located over a widespread area and there is a variety of methods of data transmission that can be employed in the data gathering (see previous comments).

Still ranking as one of the best methods available and covering the whole of the UK is the Post Office service. Where the gathering of information is not too time critical then care should be taken to avoid installing unnecessarily sophisticated and expensive on-line data capture devices. Using the postal service, input forms or extracts can be sent to the central point or points where they are converted into machine readable form and then processed. There are a variety of machine readable transcription methods e.g. punching, pre-encoded documents, mark-sensing, use of portable terminals fitted with tape cassettes. It is necessary to examine closely the various alternative methods available before choosing the appropriate method of gathering sales data.

Where the volume and cost can be justified then data links via Post Office telephone lines might be employed. There is a variety of line speeds coupled with different time slot availabilities which can cater for a variety of needs.

Forecasts of developments in the late 1970s indicate that there will be a vast expansion in the use of remote terminals. These may or may not have some local intelligence incorporated within them. They may or may not be linked via a leased line or may use the switched public network. There is a considerable amount of research and development work considering the way in which the speeds of these various peripheral devices and their linkage methods may be further improved. All this is leading towards the more general adoption of centralised processing on a medium to large computer with input and output access available via a network. In addition to the conventional keyboard terminal there are many instances where a local slow speed printing device can be used and this possibility should not be ruled out for actual printing of invoices. If it is felt that salesmen can with advantage deliver the invoices then it may be worthwhile organising the local printing of up-to-date invoices and statements to justify calls being made on customers by sales representatives.

In summary the computer facilities available assist the adoption of business plans which favour decentralisation of 'field activities'.

CONTROL

It has been mentioned before that a well-organised computer system can provide the means for a much tighter control of debtors' records than the use of more conventional means. A user manager would expect that the service he is paying for from the data processing department would be backed by the necessary professionalism and expertise and that the *appropriate methods of control* would prevail throughout all the sections of the data processing activity.

The user department staff must be deeply involved throughout the testing of a new system and also in the check-out of all modifications to the programs. The methods of control to be employed should be examined. Any operational lapse resulting in relaxation of the degree of control will bring about a deterioration in cash flow and bad debts.

From time to time it will be worthwhile to employ an independent agency to examine the control methods. One way to do this is to ensure that these aspects of the yearly audit of accounts concentrate upon the control standards laid down and more particularly upon the way in which they are carried out on a day-to-day basis.

SECURITY/BACK-UP OF HARDWARE AND SOFTWARE

Here again the user manager should be able to rely upon local expertise to ensure that the appropriate standards are followed. Once again the use of an independent examination body can make a worthwhile check. Perhaps on a biennial basis the data processing consultancy arm of the company's professional auditors could be commissioned to undertake a physical security assignment. In such a case the following terms of reference might be used: (i) physical security of the installation; (ii) security of data; (iii) the system of internal control; (iv) the records and methods of documentation; and (v) amendments to operational systems and programs. The auditors' report would be addressed to the financial controller and would provide him with an independent assessment of the adequacy of the systems currently employed. By using an independent team, the company would get the benefit of the similar exercises carried out by the team members in other companies and installations.

MISCELLANEOUS

Use of Packages

In addition to the development and availability of local custom-built, in-house systems, all financial managers must be aware of the availability of an increasing number of general purpose systems. The state of the art has led to the development of a wide range of financial packages. In some cases these can be purchased/leased to be run on the company's own computer: in other cases, the accessibility via a time-sharing terminal may be adequate. Packages, because of their general purpose nature, suffer from this aspect of generality. Nevertheless there does exist some measure of local flexibility and usually systems allow for the prompt availability of reports etc. It should be borne in mind that you are getting the benefits of several years of systems development for a share of the costs. This point naturally brings out the use of time-sharing terminals. In some cases modelling and simulation require very small amounts of machine time but the machines involved are of a size much greater than the everyday needs in general company terms. Terminals available on a switched line, say to the ATLAS Computer Bureau, should be seriously considered.

Improved Staff Efficiency / Morale

Every opportunity should be taken to computerise the more routine types of jobs. The resultant areas requiring continuing clerical control should be of a nature that provides a significantly higher degree of job satisfaction. This in turn will be reflected in the reduction in recruitment and staff training costs.

Auditors / Shareholders

At various times during the year, particularly at the year-end, the company's auditors will require evidence of the 'control of cash'. Here again a properly organised data control system maintained on a computer should considerably simplify everyone's work. There are now available a number of computer systems that are used by auditing firms to extract their own information from computer files thereby proving independently the efficiency of the control system.

COMPUTERISED DEBTORS' FILES

File Structure

From time to time the importance of the information stored within the computer files has been stressed. Over and above this factor, it is important to try to identify the extent to which the financial accounting system, or a debtors' control system, is being computerised. Whilst the latter inevitably forms a vital part of the former, particularly in companies where large systems are required for the maintenance of domestic accounting records, the relationship between the two needs may require a hierarchy of files and it must be debated whether or not this hierarchy might best be maintained outside the computer system.

The primary decision is whether or not to computerise the 'financial ledger accounts'. Many financial controllers hold the view that they would prefer to have the flexibility at month-ends and particularly at year-ends of making the necessary transfers without the constraints of input /authority /report production imposed by a rigid computer system. Where this is the case then each of the appropriate parts of the computer system might well be maintained separately as follows:

1. Debtors' control system

2. Payroll/salary administration system

3. Invoices/disbursements system

4. Financial modelling system e.g. for monitoring effects of variations in cash flow

The arguments for and against flexibility once again need consideration. The more inter-related the various aspects, the less the resultant flexibility. As in all things the decisions will depend upon the general organisational structure of the company or group.

File Design/Content

There are a number of ways of organising the computer-based debtors' files. The size and cost of the appropriate system will depend upon local circumstances. The four most critical factors are:

1. The number of account records to be maintained

2. The amount of data per record to be stored and this is significantly influenced by the percentage of accounts which may at any time be in arrears

3. The cycle of payments e.g. monthly, quarterly

4. The types of customers e.g. a large file of domestic customer records would be supported by an entirely different system from that which one would use for a file of industrial/commercial debtors

The decision whether or not to store the information on disc or magnetic tape would depend upon the factors mentioned above together with the outcome of the decision on 'access methods'. If prompt access to up-to-date files is needed then disc storage could be cost justified.

The user manager need not be concerned with the detailed design considerations but he may be interested to know how his computer manager has decided to set up the system.

1. Single master file. In this instance all the data, both personal and financial etc., would be held on one continuous record. This might facilitate access to any part of the information stored within the record.

2. Sectionalised file. The file may be divided into and accessible by sections such as:

a. Personal details e.g. names and addresses (branch/company/group)

b. Financial details e.g. amounts of debits by separate transactions; payments made, accrued interest calculated, discounts allowed

c. Management information in abbreviated form e.g. coded information of geographical area and merchandise definition, with accumulated year-to-date totals

Individual Debtors' Records

The manner in which the information is organised would depend upon the overall structure /design agreed and influenced also by the storage medium (disc or tape). The user manager need not concern himself with the efficiency of the method chosen to 'pack the data' or to organise the 'header blocks' but must be very concerned to satisfy himself that the type of information to be stored /retrieved will enable the debtors' control system to assist the company's cash flow effectively.

Cross-referencing

Where a system is needed to maintain a large number of debtors' records then the choice exists whether or not to index these on either (i) a customer basis i.e. *all* debtors' transaction /sales accounts aggregated together, or (ii) a transaction basis i.e. each different sale being recorded separately.

In many ways the second alternative would prove to be the simpler and may well meet the required needs. Where, however, it is necessary to know the aggregate indebtedness of a customer and indeed to be able to apportion payments received to the accounts in arrears, then the first choice would be an advantage. Various systems of cross-referencing debts are available. One extra debtor's account might incorporate the separate transaction references for each new account /debt incurred. These can then be chained together to produce an aggregate balance.

CONVERSION

When designing a new computer system it may well be necessary to consider how best to interface with or take over from the existing system.

In simple terms there are two options: one can allow the accounts records on the old system to simply die away, and to employ the new system only in support of future new sales. Alternatively a date can be chosen and the existing records balanced and converted into the new style, content and format, and then subsequently maintained by the new computer system. In many circumstances there will be no particular problem in deciding which of these two main alternatives should be chosen.

If there are large numbers of records involved e.g. half a million, then it will be worthwhile to undertake a brief feasibility study to determine the operational problems and costs involved under either method.

With the introduction of a new system there are inevitably many, many problems. These problems will arise in spite of the best laid plans. Such problems will obviously be compounded by the need to run two different systems alongside each other albeit for the different records or different areas of debtor system. Ideally, under these circumstances, one should reduce to the minimum the period of overlap. Where the number of debtor records is several hundred thousand then it may indeed be a physical impossibility to convert the complete file at one instant.

The job of conversion from old to new will probably be spread over a number of months and care must be taken to determine how best to sectionalise the transfer. It might be borne in mind that the first ledger/section/region to be transferred will be to an extent a guinea-pig. Within the planning time scale a suitable gap should be left following the operational conversion of this first area to allow all concerned sufficient time to gain the operational experience! Time might also usefully be taken to make any further program changes resulting from the experience gained on this first section.

A further point is the timing of the conversion exercise. If possible one should avoid periods of high summer when holidays are being taken and clerical sections are under-strength. One should avoid clashing with other 'changes' e.g. decimalisation, metrication or a physical move of location. If it is not possible to avoid such a clash, special care needs to be taken in the planning.

It is found on a number of occasions that this whole area of conversion is neglected. The design staff concerned become pre-occupied with the benefits that will be gained from the use of the new system. It is possible that a separate suite of computer programs will need to be designed, written and tested just for conversion. Where the nature of the old and new methods of processing are substantially different, there may need to be a considerable amount of clerical pre-coding work. This would involve taking the old style records in whatever form and preparing them for transfer. Whilst engaged on the usual forms of sectional balancing the opportunity should be taken to insert the multitude of pieces of coded information that the new computer system is going to rely upon.

Reference was made in the section on 'debtors' file content' to the various pieces of personal and statistical information. Particularly where the file is of a large size such information will be stored in coded form and will probably need to be entered into the system in coded form. Many decisions will need to be taken on the problems involved in trying to create computer records for those converted accounts e.g. should an attempt be made to input a full range of required information?

CASH PAYMENTS

In support of the flow outwards of cash, the various computer systems available can facilitate the use of automated money transmission systems in very much the same way as was described in the preceding section dealing with cash receipts. It is obvious to the reader that the 'payments' of one company are the 'receipts' of another. The main objective of the exercise is to try to ensure that your company is maximising the use of the appropriate money transmission methods.

Before dealing with the particular types of payment e.g. salaries and wages, it is worthwhile examining the benefits that can be derived from the use of a computerised expenses control system. Having identified the profit centres and cost centres of the company, each of these should formulate a financial plan for at least the current accounting year. In many instances such a plan is formulated for three, five or even ten years. For each of the cost centres there would be the appropriate system of estimating and then approving the likely expenditure analysed under the appropriate sub-accounts. The computer support system would receive as input data the details of actual payments made i.e. payroll, invoices etc. By use of a coding system, these outgoings would be matched against the stored, planned figures and variances listed. For those areas of out-goings that were covered by such a budget control system, this alone might well provide an adequate mechanism for controlling and monitoring cash payments. Except in cases where the amounts were of significant proportion, the results from this system could well be sufficient. Naturally there would be some short-comings and it might be necessary to develop the use of a more sophisticated cash flow control system. In concept this would be along the same lines as an expenses budget system but with the emphasis on cash flow.

Cash outgoings can be simply categorised as:

1. Payroll: payments of salaries and wages

2. Invoices: payments for goods and external services

3. Self-generated payments: stockholders' interest, leases, rents, etc.

PAYROLL

The case for the justification of computerising the payroll has been made many times over the past years. In the case where the payment structure is simple, the computer takes over what is otherwise a routine clerical chore. Where there are complicated wage rate structures, the computer system is capable of dealing with the multitude of variances and in carrying out all calculations and analyses quickly in order that the weekly pay-day deadlines can be met.

Payment by Bank Transfer

Where the actual payment of wages and salaries is to be made by bank transfer, then various systems are available to enable this to be done on a computer basis. Some need the production of individual payment vouchers; other systems allow for the transfer of cash by magnetic tape. As with any other computer to computer system, many problems are minimised:

a. The cost and security risks involved in handling physical cash are eliminated

b. Payment dates can be varied e.g. greater flexibility is available at holiday times. Where it is to the company's advantage and still within the terms of the contract of employment, payment/transfer dates can be arranged to time the actual transfer of funds between the manager's bank account and the banker's computer system to suit the company's cash flow policy

c. Where the payment is made by Bank Giro Credit through the Bankers' Automated Clearing Services, then the credits to the bank accounts of members of staff are balanced by the *one* debit to the company's account i.e. there will not be a corresponding number of individual debit entries. This may allow for a significant reduction in bank charges

Payment by Cash/Cheque

A computerised payroll system can more readily provide the necessary analysis of cash required for payment vouchers/cheques with maximum flexibility.

SALARY ADMINISTRATION

In many organisations, the annual payroll payments are a very significant proportion of the total outgoings. It is vital for the company to know, particularly in times of high inflation rates, what their future cash flow commitments will be. The amounts involved can materially affect the present and future company liquidity and profitability position. This aspect of the 'computerised payroll' is equally as important in terms of salary administration and assisting in the control of the flow of money as in the routine weekly or monthly payroll production exercise.

With the computerisation of salary administration records a data base exists which enables a company to extract promptly both historical and projected information which will have a considerable bearing upon esti- mated cash flow. The information can be made available in the form of reports, graphs, charts and visual displays. The content of the output is only limited by the amount and type of information captured and stored. It is possible to derive details of the following functions:

Salary administration. These are future cost patterns, effects of inflation, effects of possible wage awards and indeed any other information derivable from the information stored or a projection upon that information e.g. differential patterns within functional areas.

Manpower analysis and planning.   This is perhaps the most important area of information available from a computerised salary administration system. Again depending upon the information stored, future projections can be made concerning the manpower needs and obviously the effect upon cash flow.

Pensions administration.   Where the company operates a non-contributory pension scheme, a salary administration data base provides the essential information for considering the adequacy of the rates of contribution. There is also the area of payment of pensions. The extent to which existing pension payments require to become index-related would provide a relatively straightforward job when carried out by computer in projecting information held upon the 'pensions data base'.

Income tax/national insurance payments.   In addition to the outgoings in terms of payments to staff, more accurate and up-to-date information is available regarding the future income tax and national insurance payments. Once again these amounts, and in particular the employer's contributions for national insurance purposes, can be analysed and projected for the months and years ahead.

·It is once again apparent that an essential feature common to all these aspects and facilities of a salary administration system is the need to get maximum relevant information stored within the data base. Bearing in mind as always the problems of initially capturing and subsequently amending the information, a large amount of time needs to be spent in setting up the content of the information to be stored within the computer. It is important to decide not only what information shall be stored but also the type of 'history' information e.g. relating to salary/wage increases previously granted.

The classical situation arises whereby, from a computerised data base, not only is a routine administrative type of job capable of being carried out tidily, e.g. payroll production, but also much information is available for extraction and analysis which vitally affects the control of the flow of money.

INVOICES

Once again it is necessary to recognise the overall facilities available from the use of a computerised expenses control system. Following the appropriate authorisation for payment of invoices for goods and services, one remaining problem of significance is the timing of making the payment.

It is possible, although not necessarily cost justified in all circumstances, to distinguish by computer program the relative cost advantages of:

a. Prompt payment of invoices in order to obtain preferential discounts

b. Deferment of payment of invoices so as to enjoy the use of funds for a slightly longer period

The answer to both of these questions requires the availability of the cost of many money factors and is inevitably bound up with the company's overall liquidity situation. Depending upon the amounts involved, the method of funding and the costs of borrowing, there can be considerable profit and loss type savings available from the use of a system to calculate the optimum timing of the payment of invoices. This factor has latterly attracted considerable attention and there has been a noticeable delay in invoice payment i.e. a slowing down in the transfer of funds. The consideration of VAT inflow and outflow can be determined and the company's net liability position struck. It is obvious that further control aspects are available which have a bearing upon cash flow when a company is equipped with a computerised stock control system. Payment of invoices for goods taken into stock can be influenced by optimising stock levels and consequently purchases.

SELF-GENERATED PAYMENTS

Some examples of this type of commitment are interest payments, payments on leases etc. In many cases the onus for payment is with the debtor and he has probably very little flexibility within the terms of the agreement, lease etc.

Within the overall purchasing policy laid down by a company might be found guidelines covering the arguments on rent, lease or purchase. In adddition to the problems of cash flow there are other financial and tax considerations. Nevertheless the contribution to cash flow that can stem from exercising an option to lease should not be ignored. There are available a number of computer packages which will show the effects e.g. on cash flow of various options. It is necessary to identify the principal input parameters governed by the various circumstances. These are then fitted into the appropriate computer program and the user is supplied with various responses indicating the effects of the alternative courses of action.

CASH MANAGEMENT POLICIES IN GENERAL

Principles should be unshakeable. Policies are influenced by the 'weighting of the factors'. There are very many factors governing a company's cash management policy. We are not intending to comment deeply upon the subject of the next chapter i.e. upon the use of money. However we think that the comments made earlier within this chapter need to be set against the overall 'liquidity movement' of the company i.e. the sources from which cash is received and the manner in which that cash has been disposed of. Where the yearly amounts of the cash receipts and payments are significant, fluctuating and subject to external influences, they must be supported by the best possible 'control system'. We maintain that a properly designed computer system that has been and continues to be closely involving its user managers offers the best means of providing that control.

CHAPTER 5

The Control of the Use of Money

BY I. HANDYSIDE

Business is an economic activity and the essence of business enterprise is economic performance. The reputation of a business as far as the general public is concerned is derived from the quality of its products or services; the success of a business, on the other hand, is measured by economic performance. At the end of the day a business is assessed in financial terms of profits made and return on capital employed.

Managers are those people in a business who are responsible for the use of resources, and the primary task of managers is to manage those resources under their control in the most effective way possible. The term 'effective management' is now common but it was not very long ago that the emphasis was on 'efficient management'. In his essay on the effective business, Drucker explains the reasoning behind the change. He prefers 'effective' because the real key to effective management 'is the factor of giving attention to the right things'. He sees 'efficiency', on the other hand, as 'being concerned to do things rightly', adding the interesting comment that many people are doing things 'efficiently' that need not be done at all!

The British Institute of Management has been pressing the need for action in developing effective management performance, and to this end has produced a document identifying the major areas where managers need most help at individual level. One of the most important areas is the primary need for managers to understand and use financial information in order to improve their decision-making capability: in defining problems, generating options and collecting relevant information as the basis of good decisions. The manager's need for prompt and relevant information is becoming vital with the increasing complexities of modern business, economic pressures and the pace of social and legislative changes.

This chapter is concerned with how managers can use a computer as a primary tool for the control of financial resources. The computer is the means of providing managers with the information necessary for them to make the best possible use of the resources for which they are responsible. Accountancy has been called the language of business, and the basis of management information is accounting information because in a business in the final analysis it is economic performance that matters. The type of information managers need varies from company to company, and between different levels of management; but in all business and at all levels, managers have most need of good information for the effective planning and controlling of the use of financial resources (working capital) and financial performance (cash flow).

FINANCIAL PERFORMANCE: CASH FLOW

Financial accounts have provided the main source of information used by managers for operating decisions or in the assessment of performance. Standard financial accounting systems, however, provide a type and content of information which is more concerned with the external requirements of a business: with shareholders, creditors and tax inspectors, for instance, than with the internal requirements of managers. The task of the financial accountant is to record the details of income and expenditure in such a way that the overall trading position of a business can be reported at a given time. Although of limited value for planning and controlling activities, this information is nevertheless fundamental and must form the basis of any internal management information system.

FINANCIAL RESOURCES: WORKING CAPITAL

Apart from manpower, the resources for which managers are responsible, converted into financial terms, add up to the money required to support the sales of products or services of a business enterprise, in other words the working capital; and the function of good information is to help managers reduce the level of working capital needed to support a given level of sales so as to provide surplus cash for investment and expansion.

The main elements of working capital for which adequate cash resources must be available are:

1. Stocks: raw materials, work-in-progress and finished goods
2. Debtors: cash due from sales
3. Creditors: supplies of material and services, wages and salaries, and overheads

In financial accounting terms, stocks and debtors, together with cash balances, make up current assets, and creditors, current liabilities. The relationship of the elements of working capital is illustrated in Figure 5.1, which also gives a good illustration of the flow of cash in a manufacturing business.

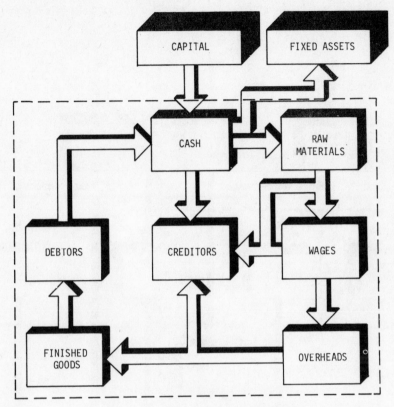

Figure 5.1   Elements of Working Capital

For service industries, the item of raw materials (which in the diagram would include work-in-progress) would not be appropriate, and the element of finished goods would read finished services.

The vital importance of keeping abreast with and in control of the current state of each of the elements of working capital was made forcibly by a managing director recently in a paper presented to fellow directors at a conference. His task had been to haul the company from red ink into the black of profit.* He said, 'It is also a must to be building for tomorrow, while struggling to survive today. This may be the most difficult thing to do while funds are short. It involves spending badly needed cash on engineering and marketing, and on professional detailed accounting. The financial position must be in the briefcase every week, however far the case and its owner are from home, including details like invoicing due this week, orders due and cash flow.'

---

* *Management Today*, April 1975

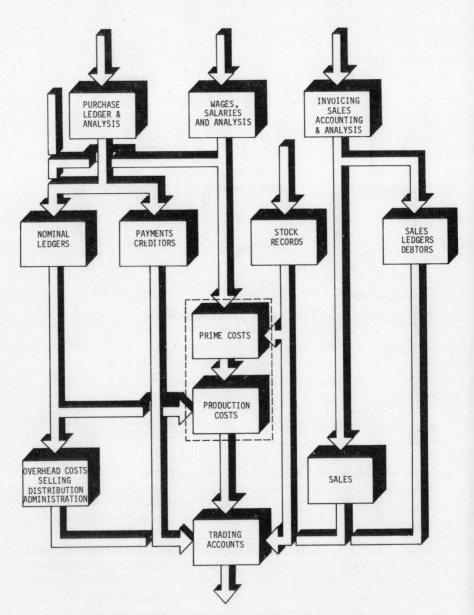

Figure 5.2   Outline of Computer-based Financial Accounting System

DATA PROCESSING METHODS

Data processing methods have been used to provide financial accounting information from the early days of punched card machines. The systems were necessarily simple but nonetheless effective in providing accurate data for accountants to prepare regular statements to managers of the financial position of the business. The procedures were separate and generally unrelated but covered the basic elements of working capital: (i) invoicing and sales ledgers; (ii) purchase ledger and analysis; (iii) nominal ledger and analysis; (iv) wages; and (v) stock records.

The regular statements produced from these early systems at least provided managers with basic control on creditors, debtors and stocks. With the increasing complexity of modern business, managers have been demanding information specifically directed to their own needs. This demand proved difficult and expensive to satisfy until the advent of the modern commercial computer systems. Computers with their powerful facilities for storage and manipulation of data, and the rapid developments made, and being made, in computer hardware, software and communications systems have made available to managers a facility for providing a range of detailed and selective information that would have been not only impracticable but also prohibitive in terms of cost no more than a few years ago.

Through using computers many businesses have developed over a short period of time comprehensive accounting systems with a degree of integration of related data, providing managers with purposeful information selected for their own particular requirements. Figure 5.2 illustrates in outline form a computer-based financial accounting and costing system which, with one or two minor variations, is widely used by manufacturing industries.

The financial accounting and costing system illustrated is based on six sub-systems which collect and process all the day-to-day transactions of the business. At the end of each financial period, the data is collated and summarised to prepare the trading accounts. The sub-systems are listed in Figure 5.3.

When the accounts are closed down at the end of the accounting period, data representing the period of transactions from each system is held on computer files. The data is then summarised and processed to provide management control reports and trading accounts. The build-up of trading accounts from the summarised data of each system is illustrated in Figure 5.4.

The type of information and the degree of detail provided by the sort of financial accounting system illustrated depends on the accounting structure and costing system used. It is no part of the purpose of this chapter to discuss the merits or disadvantages of various accounting

Sub-system	Input	Output
Purchase Ledger and Analysis	Suppliers' Invoices	Payments to Suppliers
		Control of Creditors
		Purchase Allocations
Wages, Salaries and Payroll Analysis	Wages Sheets	Payment of Wages and Salaries
	Salary Data	Payrolls and Payroll Analysis for Allocation of Wages and Salaries
Invoicing, Sales Accounting and Sales Analysis	Orders, Deliveries	Customer Invoices
	Cash Receipts	Sales Ledgers
		Debtor Control
		Analysis of Sales
Stock Records (Raw Materials, Work-in-progress, Finished Goods)	Receipts from Purchase Ledger System and from Production	Stock Balances
		Stock Control
	Issues to Production and Deliveries to Customers	
Nominal Ledger	Sales, Distribution and Administration Expenses	Expenditure Analysis
		Expenditure Allocation
	Production Overheads	
	Depreciation	
Production Costing	Data for Direct Labour and Material	Production Costs
		Production Costs
	Production Overheads	

Figure 5.3   Financial Accounting Sub-systems

and coding structures, but it must be said that accounting structures and coding systems play a crucial role in the type and detail of information provided by business systems, and this is particularly applicable with regard to computer-based systems. It is not an exaggeration to state that coding is the key to data processing; for transmitting, manipulating,

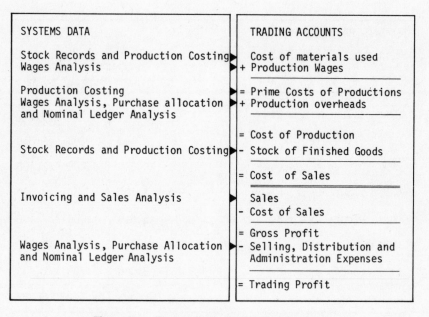

Figure 5.4   Systems Input for Trading Accounts

storing, selecting and retrieving information. For this reason accounting structures and coding systems of any business must be based on a real understanding of how financial and management information is required to flow through the business, and what types and levels of reports are required: who needs the information and in how much detail. The data that is needed about transactions fall into three main categories:

1. To identify, name, specify and classify
2. To indicate the source or origin
3. To indicate relationships between transactions

The accounting structure and coding system used must make possible the accurate recording of the day-to-day transaction of the business in such a way as to provide the means to present selected results to managers, both financial and operating, in adequate detail.

Figures 5.5 and 5.6 illustrate levels of detail provided by a coding system. The examples are taken from the expenditure analysis report provided each period from the financial accounting system discussed earlier. They are used by the manager responsible, in this case the financial director.

ADMINISTRATION EXPENSES				PERIOD 5	
DEPT 14	CENTRAL ACCOUNTS				
CODE	EXPENSE	PREVIOUS YEAR			
		PERIOD	TO DATE	PERIOD	TO DATE
		£	£	£	£
3100	Salaries & wages	10.800	53.600	14.500	68.500
3200	Travelling expenses	800	4.100	850	4.800
3300	Office expenses	5.700	26.500	6.400	32.400
3400	Light, heat, power	500	3.100	600	3.800
3500	Occupancy costs	1.200	6.500	1.200	7.100
3600	Equipment costs	2.500	12.000	4.200	19.700
3900	Sundry expenses	400	2.000	700	2.700
		21.900	107.800	28.450	139.000

Figure 5.5   Summary of Administration Expenses

The information presented in Figures 5.5 and 5.6 is interesting and of some value but it is hardly useful as a basis for control. Comparisons with previous years' results are no indication of effectiveness or performance as the conditions prevailing in each year could be very different. There are no target comparisons, which are the real basis for control and control reporting is the basis of all effective management information systems. Most managers would agree that if they could closely and frequently monitor the activities under their control, they could achieve better levels of performance. To assist managers, control systems of one sort or another are needed to signal conditions which require management intervention.

Standard financial accounting and costing systems are concerned with historical facts and, as such, have limited use in management planning and control functions. The development of management accounting, although derived from traditional financial accounting and costing techniques, is a significant change of emphasis in the role of accounting information. In fact, management accounting is the application of accounting techniques to provide information specifically for planning and controlling business activities. Financial accounting is to do with stewardship

ADMINISTRATION EXPENSES		PREVIOUS
DEPT 14 CENTRAL ACCOUNTS		
CODE 31 SALARIES & WAGES		
CODE	EXPENSE	PREVIOUS PERIOD
		£
11	Managers	
12	Secretarial	
20	Accounting staff	
21	Supervisors	
22	Clerical	
30	Computer staff	
31	Systems	
32 .	Programming	
33	Operations	
34	Data preparation	
91	Pensions & Nat.Ins.	
92	Recruitment & Training	

Figure 5.6   Analysis of Salaries and Wages Expenditure

(profit and loss accounts and balance sheets); management accounting is to do with control, providing information at regular intervals in such a way that actual performance can be compared with budgets, and any differences analysed by causes.

The primary tools of the management accountant are budgetary control and standard costing. In his book *Financial Management Handbook*, A. R. Leaper identifies five reasons for using a formalised system of budgetary control:

1. It defines the objective of an organisation as a whole and in financial terms

2. It provides a yardstick for measuring performance

3. It reveals the extent by which actual results have varied from the desired objective

4. It provides a guide for corrective action

5. It allows responsiblilty to be delegated whilst maintaining centralised control

BUDGETARY CONTROL

Budgetary control involves preparing a plan for the business in financial terms. The plan usually starts with the forecast of sales (the sales budget), which is then converted into a production budget which, in turn, is broken down into the estimated expenditure necessary for labour, materials and other expenses to meet the production target. Additional expenditure is estimated for administration and other overhead expenses to support the planned level of sales and production, and expressed in terms of budgets. These various steps in the preparation of budgets eventually lead to the compilation of a budgeted profit and loss account.

To monitor the actual results of business operations, the budgets are broken down into convenient periods of time (usually accounting periods) and compared with the actual income and expenditure for that period. The differences between actual results and budgeted estimates are called 'variances'.

While such comparisons are useful, their value to managers is limited if the comparisons reveal only major differences between actual and budgeted expenditure. The real value to managers of budgetary control procedures lies in the level of detail in which budgets are compared. The more detailed the budget and the analysis of the actual results, the more valuable is the information to managers as an instrument of control, not only because it is easier to isolate responsibility, but also because the causes of variances are more easily identified and the reason for their occurrence understood, so that action can be taken either to prevent unfavourable variances re-occurring, or to exploit favourable conditions.

Nevertheless, standard budgetary control procedures on their own provide no more than a blunt instrument of control. The value of budgetary control systems lies not only in the detail provided but also in the manner and arithmetic used to prepare the forecast expenditure. Estimates for items of expenditure are 'budgeted costs' which are generally an anticipation of what the actual expenditure would be, rather than what it *should* be at the most efficient level of activity. As a result the control aspect becomes rather academic as performance in terms of output and efficiency is virtually ignored.

Budgeted costs of this sort are generally used for overhead expenses, such as administration expenses, and because of the nature of overhead expenses do provide an adequate instrument of control. They are, however, of limited value as a means of controlling production costs or the cost of service activities where it is necessary, for control purposes, to measure performance in terms of output and efficiency. For this reason, standard costing techniques were introduced.

STANDARD COSTING

Standard Costing was developed from the needs of modern industrial managers:

1. To cost and price products and services in advance of manufacture or work
2. To plan and schedule manufacturing, services and marketing operations
3. To control operating results

Standard costs have been defined as the anticipated costs of a specific product or service at a given level of volume and under an assumed set of circumstances; and is derived not only from accounting principles and procedures, but from engineering and work-study techniques for developing methods, standards and operating procedures. Allied to budgetary control, standard costing has been accepted as a vital tool for management planning and control. It involves establishing standards for each expense directly incurred in producing a product or service. A 'standard' defines, as scientifically as possible, what will be required in terms of effort, quantity and costs, under assumed conditions of efficiency and level of output, to provide a certain volume of goods or services, covering such factors as rates of pay, man hours, machine rates and hours, and material costs. Standard costing records exactly what is done in the same way as budgetary control forecasts what should be done. Because comparisons are made against a pre-determined standard, expense by expense, the resulting variances can be analysed by cause to provide meaningful information to managers.

The difficulties experienced in introducing standard costing and budgetary control procedures have primarily been associated with the amount of data involved. To introduce sophisticated control procedures without using a computer in some form is inconceivable in this day and age. The computer overcomes the difficulties of manipulating large volumes of data for control reports quickly, accurately and economically, and in a level of detail that is impracticable by other methods. For this reason, computers are being used increasingly, not only by large organisations but also by small businesses to open up new approaches to control information, rather than merely to speed up and improve the accuracy and detail of financial systems.

It has been said that all internal activities of a business result in costs, and it is the control of these costs that is one of the prime objectives of budgetary control.

COSTING SYSTEMS

Basic cost accounting is concerned with recording, classifying and allocating costs by: (i) function—production, selling, distribution and administration; (ii) cost elements—wages, materials, and expenses; (iii) classification —direct, indirect and overhead expenses.

There are two main types of costing system: job costing and process costing. In a job costing system, costs are compiled for making a specific product (or batch of products) or service. The cost unit remains an identifiable unit as it passes through the production process, and the costs, directly associated with the job or batch, plus a calculated or estimated portion of overhead expenses, are changed to the specific job. Process costing systems, on the other hand, are used in those industries (milk processing and cement manufacture are examples) where large quantities of similar units or products are produced by continuous methods. For process costing systems it is neither useful nor practicable to identify batches of production for cost accounting purposes. The emphasis is on the accumulation of costs for all work units during a period of time. At the end of each period the cost per unit of goods produced is determined as an average of all the unit costs for the period.

These costs, however, are historical costs and are of limited value to managers as a yardstick for measuring efficiency. In a standard costing system, the historical costs are set against and compared with predetermined costs and the differences analysed to indicate to the managers responsible where the variations to plan are occurring, and for what reasons.

The computer is the ideal, if not the only, medium for carrying out budgetary control and standard costing work because of its facilities for storing and manipulating large volumes of data. An example of a computer system for budgetary control and standard costing is illustrated in diagram form at Figure 5.7.

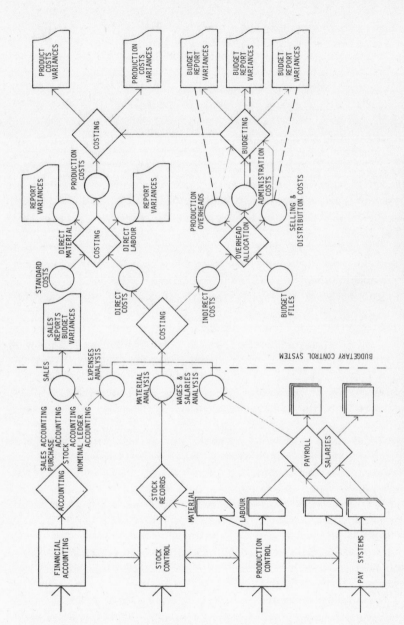

Figure 5.7 Budgetary Control and Standard Costing System

AN EXAMPLE OF A COMPUTER SYSTEM FOR BUDGETARY CONTROL AND STANDARD COSTING

This example is taken from a computer system used by a company in the process manufacturing industry. Management control information is developed from the computer systems for the payment of wages and salaries, production and stock control and financial accounting. These basic systems were originally designed as independent and unrelated procedures to satisfy particular needs of management. As part of an overall plan for budgetary control, they were subsequently developed and linked into an integrated system.

Transactions are processed daily for each of the basic systems for purposes of invoicing, updating stock records, suppliers' payments, payment of wages and salaries, production scheduling and control. The transaction data is accumulated and stored in the computer's files of each basic system until the end of the accounting period.

The use of computers for production and material control is the subject of a later chapter and, therefore, in the context of the budgetary control system it is necessary only to mention the main output from these systems, i.e. volumes of production and labour and material costs.

Factory employee job cards from input for factory payroll procedures and, together with attendance records and amendment data, are used to calculate pay and bonus. As part of the payroll system, the job cards relating to production processes are costed by reference to employee pay rates stored in the payroll master files, and together with other factory wages data is stored for subsequent input into the costing procedures. A similar procedure applies to pay systems for office wages and monthly salaries which are analysed by function and cost code and stored for subsequent allocation.

Material issues, extended at standard costs, result from the production control and stock control systems. Receipts into stock derive from the purchase accounting system and from production control data. The purchase accounting system produces periodic reports for the purchasing manager, showing variances between actual and standard costs of materials supplied. From these reports the purchasing manager can see the trend of prices and pinpoint significant variances. These may necessitate re-negotiation with suppliers in terms of order quantities and discounts, or seeking alternative sources of supply at lower cost, or adjustments to standard costs.

The output data from the financial accounting system for the purposes of budgetary control concern sales and expenditure analysis. The expenses are accumulated from data resulting from purchase accounting and nominal ledger procedures. Expenses include such items as supplies, power, heat and light, telephone and office expenses, travelling and hotel expenses, company transport and cars, advertising, charges for Professional and other services, repairs and maintenance of plant and buildings, insurance, rental charges, rates and depreciation. These expense items together with the payroll and salaries charges form the total expenses of the business for the period.

At the end of each accounting period, the financial accounts are processed and trial balances produced. The detailed transaction data which have been accumulated during the processing of accounting procedures are collated and sorted by location, department and cost code and stored for subsequent allocation.

Data from the production control and stock control systems relating to material usage and costs (at standard costs) are combined with the direct production wages data selected from the wages analysis file to process direct material and labour costs for production processes and products. The production and product master files hold standard cost specifications for a given volume of production or, in the case of products, a unit cost rate for material and labour. By referring to the standard costs, cost statements are prepared for production processes showing comparisons against standard and indicating variances where these occur. The computer is programmed to highlight (by a special symbol) only those variances where the actual costs differ from standard by a given percentage. This was found necessary as small variances occurred frequently because of varying production circumstances which were normal and acceptable. Where, however, a breakdown in plant spoils a batch of material, the variance against standard would be large and in excess of the percentage margin and, therefore, highlighted by the computer as an unfavourable variance. Another example is where the introduction of new equipment for materials handling decreased the amount of allowable material waste, resulting in a favourable variance.

The indirect costs which had been selected out during the costing and allocation processing routines are combined together and then segregated by function and expense code and processed against budget files to provide budgetary control reports for each department and location within function. The production overheads data is selected out and becomes input to a further costing process to give total production costs for the period for each factory and product. This processing produces budgetary control reports based on standard costs for production and product cost.

The production overheads are those expenses incurred by production locations during the period and which cannot be directly attributed to product manufacturing processes, but which, nevertheless, are incurred to support the production processes. These expenses include:

a. The salaries and wages of factory managers, and supervisory, inspection, maintenance, clerical and services staff

b. Charges for fuel, power, heat and light

c. Indirect materials

d. General expenses: office expenses, repairs and maintenance of plant and buildings, transport and travelling expenses

e. Fixed charges: insurance, rentals, rates and depreciation

These overhead costs are apportioned to product costs. The methods for apportioning overhead costs and calculating overhead absorption rates depend upon a variety of circumstances, including volumes of production. In the budgetary control system illustrated, the allocation of overhead expenses to cost centres and products is carried out manually. The automatic apportioning of overheads by computer using standard overhead absorption rates is not difficult technically, but the resulting control reports could be misleading in cases where the volume of production differed significantly from the volume level on which the single standard costs were based.

FLEXIBLE BUDGETS

To equate standard costs with levels of production, flexible budgets are used. Flexible budgets are those which are designed to provide control information for various levels of activity. In those industries where the pattern of demand is relatively stable and can be forecast with reasonable accuracy, fixed budgets are used for control purposes. There are industries however, where stable conditions do not exist and where several forecasts of demand are necessary, particularly in those industries where weather or fashion are dominating influences—ice-creams and umbrellas to name but two. To rely on a fixed budget as a standard for comparison would be unsatisfactory, as fluctuations in output could lead to violent deviations from budget, making nonsense of the comparison reports. In flexible budgeting a series of budget figures is compiled to cover a range of levels of activity, and the division of costs into fixed and variable is of critical importance in such a context. Variable costs tend to remain constant per unit of output, and fixed costs tend to remain constant in total (although large increases in the level of output could increase fixed costs). The real problem lies in calculating standards for semi-variable costs which move upwards and downwards in step formation according to output levels. In a computer system the standard cost files would hold a series of costs, one for each level of production. During processing the actual costs would be compared with standard costs computed for the level of output attained. In terms of systems definition, decision rules and logic, those computer systems processing flexible budgets are complex.

EXPENSE ALLOCATION

The expenses associated with the selling and distribution (sales and marketing departments, transport and warehousing) and administration functions (central management and services, that is accounting and costing departments, computer and management services, personnel and pay administration, public relations and professional services) are allocated by expense code in varying degrees of detail. The actual expenses are compared against the planned budget amounts and variances reported. As mentioned earlier, standard costing techniques are not generally applicable to the sales and administration functions.

Figure 5.5 illustrated a control report for administration expenses resulting from a standard financial accounting system. Figure 5.8 illustrates how the same report would be presented by the budgetary control system.

A comparison of the reports illustrated in Figures 5.5 and 5.8 will highlight the vital role that budgets play in control information. In the example in Figure 5.8 significant overspending has occurred in two areas of expense in the Central Accounts Department: for salaries and wages, and office expenses. The reasons for over-expenditure can perhaps be easily justified—increased work load necessitating additional staff and accommodation—but the important point is that differences to plan indicate a need for some action on the part of the manager responsible.

The level of detail produced by a computer system can be extensive and judgement must be exercised by managers and their computer advisers on the type and content of control reports. Some computer systems used for budgetary control provide the managers with detailed statements of costs and variances, together with summaries of costs and variances. Where a summary variance is significant, the manager can turn to the detailed statements to determine the cause of difference. Other computer systems provide managers with summary cost statements and variances, and provide further analysis only on request. Whichever method is chosen depends on the requirements of managers and on convenience, timing and cost. The important point is that each responsible manager is provided regularly with accurate comparative information on the performance of his department, and has available further and more detailed information to identify the causes of differences thus enabling him to take action to remedy or exploit a situation.

THE COST OF STOCKS

The philosophy of budgetary control is that control of resources will be accomplished more effectively by giving managers clearly defined responsibilities for the management of resources. The practice of budgetary

ADMINISTRATION EXPENSES
DEPT 14   CENTRAL ACCOUNTS

PERIOD 5

CODE	EXPENSE	PREVIOUS YEAR TO DATE	CURRENT YEAR		BUDGET TO DATE	VARIANCE
			PERIOD	TO DATE		
		£	£	£	£	£
3100	Salaries & wages	53,600	14,500	68,500	62,500	6,000 - *
3200	Travelling expenses	4,100	850	4,800	5,000	200 +
3300	Office expenses	26,500	6,400	32,400	30,000	2,400 - *
3400	Light, heat & power	3,100	600	3,800	4,000	200 +
3500	Occupancy costs	6,500	1,200	7,100	7,500	400 +
3600	Equipment costs	12,000	4,200	19,700	20,000	300 +
3900	Sundry expenses	2,000	700	2,700	2,500	200 -
		107,800	28,450	139,000	131,500	7,500 - *

Figure 5.8   Example of Budgetary Control Report

control is to provide managers with information to enable them to monitor performance and to assist them in determining what action is needed to achieve company and individual objectives. There is one major resource of a business, however, for which budgetary control by itself is not always an adequate instrument of control, and that is stock investment. Additional techniques are often required for the control of stocks. The objective of stock or inventory control is, broadly speaking, to reduce the total level of stocks to the minimum consistent with the overall objective of the company. There are difficulties in establishing optimum stock levels, and not the least of these concerns the conflicts that arise between the personal and departmental opinions of various managers on what the levels of stocks should be. Production and sales managers would naturally like stock levels pitched as high as possible in the interests of production and customer service. The accountant is conscious that stocks tie up large amounts of cash. Budgetary control systems bring to the notice of management significant imbalances in stockholding so that corrective action can be taken. But this can be a blunt instrument often resulting in arbitrary action to reduce stock with unfavourable consequent implications for production planning and customer service. Effective control of stockholdings involving a large number of items of significant value requires the application of management science techniques to find a satisfactory balance between service and cost.

Inventory control systems are based on forecasts of demand derived from the forecast of sales calculated during the preparation of budgets, which determine production activity and, therefore, the stock levels required to support the budgeted output. In Chapter 2 we saw some of the techniques for forecasting demand in inventory control systems. All the techniques attempt to calculate the trend from the recent history of demand, and use the trend to adjust the forecasts of demand for the periods ahead.

As the object of inventory control is to control the balance between stock investment and level of service, there are two principal decisions that have to be taken:

1. The order quantity, which will depend on stock level, forecast demand and the costs of stockholding

2. The time to order, which will depend on stock level, forecast demand and delivery period.

The costs associated with stockholding are acquisition costs, and holding costs, that is, interest on capital, insurance, storage costs and wages. The order quantity is calculated from mathematical formulae which take into account stockholding cost and demand forecast—the economic order quantity. The right time to order stock depends on the re-order level.

This is based on the expected usage during the period of lead time. In addition, a safety stock level is introduced as a buffer to insure against unexpected fluctuations in usage and lead time.

```
ACTION REPORT                                      PERIOD 7

STOCK ITEM                      DESCRIPTION
UNIT OF ISSUE                          DELIVERY PERIODS 3

STOCK MOVEMENTS
   PERIODS          4       5       6

   ORDERS         800
   RECEIPTS       600
   ISSUES         190     270     210
   STOCK BAL      520     250      40

DEMAND FORECAST
   PERIODS          7       8       9      10

   ORDERS         800
   RECEIPTS
   ISSUES         250     300     250     330
   STOCK BAL      590     290      40     290 - *

FORECAST ISSUES                1130
STOCK AVAILABLE                 840
MIN QUANTITY REQUIRED           290
DATE REQUIRED                  PERIOD 10
ECONOMIC ORDER QUANTITY         800
```

Figure 5.9   Inventory Control Action Report

The computer systems for inventory control vary widely in the degree of complexity in design, from basic systems calculating only the replenishment requirements to fully integrated material management systems which are discussed in a later chapter. Whatever the degree of complexity in systems design, the principal control report is the action report, an example of which is illustrated in Figure 5.9. The action report includes the demand behaviour of the stock item over previous periods, the stock balance at the beginning of the current period and the forecast demand. In the example in Figure 5.9 the forecast demand is projected over the next four periods to cover the lead time of three periods. The action needed in this case is an order for at least 290 units for delivery before period 10. From an examination of the recent demand history and the forecast usage, the Purchasing Manager would place an order immediately for the economic order quantity of 800, unless a policy decision had been made, or was being made, to increase or to decrease the current level of demand for that stock item.

Action notices are printed only for those stock items that require action of some sort so that purchasing managers are not burdened with unnecessary reports. The action taken will depend on the control information presented—the need to place additional orders as in the example above; or to bring forward planned deliveries if actual demand exceeds the forecast levels; or to delay or even cancel orders outstanding if the trend in demand is downward.

Even though the computer is accepted as an essential tool in inventory management, maximum benefit is obtained only where the pattern of stock usage is amenable to scientific forecasting techniques, and where the volumes and values of stock items justify a sophisticated control system.

Earlier in the chapter it was stated that managers have most need of good information for effectively planning and controlling the use of resources.

The use of computers to provide control information has been discussed in previous paragraphs. The natural sequence is, of course, that planning procedures are carried out first, and the resulting plans or budgets used for control purposes. It has been more convenient to discuss control systems in the first part of the chapter as in the context of computer systems development the introduction of control systems has been the natural development from standard accounting work into integrated financial and budgetary control systems. Further, the use of computers for financial planning has usually been a separate exercise, using the many packages that are available from the computer manufacturers, software houses or computer bureaux, or a later development of systems integration.

FINANCIAL PLANNING

Financial planning is part of the overall planning of a business in the long and medium term. Budgetary control is concerned with planning in the short term within the framework of the overall business plan and provides operating plans in the form of budgets which set out in financial terms the responsibilities of managers in relation to the overall policy of the business. The steps in the preparation of plans and budgets are illustrated in diagram form in Figure 5.10.

CAPITAL INVESTMENT APPRAISAL

One of the most crucial factors in the future growth and profitability of a business concerns decisions on capital expenditure. Capital investment

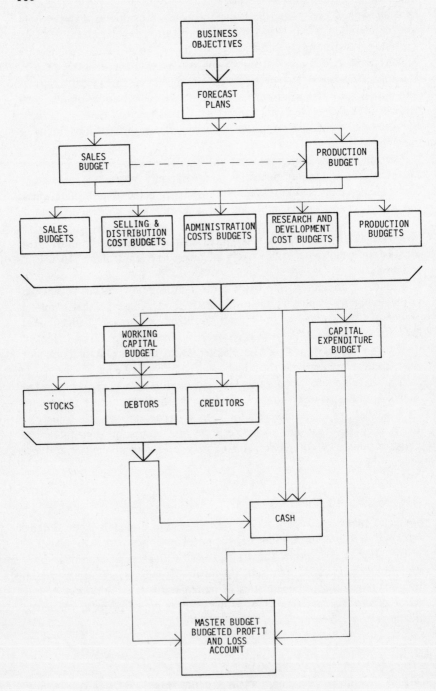

Figure 5.10   Steps in the Preparation of Plans and Budgets

appraisal and, in particular, discounted cash flow techniques are commonly used to apply more rigorous rules for evaluating how money is to be spent on new investment.

The basic objective of any investment is that for a given amount of money, a greater sum will be received back over a period of time. To obtain a true investment picture, all the cash outlays and inflows estimated to occur over the period of time selected for the investment appraisal must take account of the time when the cash outlays and inflows are planned to take place.

This is known as the 'time value of money' concept, a grand-sounding name for the simple principle that cash today has more value than cash at a future date, because of the interest that could be earned and because of inflation. This important element is the basis of the discounted cash flow method which measures cash flow in terms of its comparative value for each year, placing less value on the cash flows of later years than those of the earlier years.

The discounted cash flow technique is used in two ways:

a. To determine the rate of interest produced by a given investment (discounted cash flow or DCF) or

b. To determine the comparative value of a series of cash flows at some time in the future at a given rate of interest (present value).

Straightforward investment appraisal exercises do not need the use of a computer. Discounted yields and present values can be calculated by reference to rate tables or by the use of desk calculators. In projects, however, where large investments are to be made, there will always be imponderables which are not susceptible to measurement and evaluation in financial terms, for instance the risk inherent in a particular type of business or the sensitivity of one or two factors according to changing market conditions. In such circumstances it is not sufficient to calculate one-answer solutions for the return on capital for a large investment project, particularly when a number of variables are present.

SENSITIVITY ANALYSIS AND RISK ANALYSIS

The more sophisticated approach to investment appraisal uses computer models for 'sensitivity analysis' and 'risk analysis'. Sensitivity analysis indicates how the profitability of a project may be affected by variations or changes in an element of the project—in revenue, operating costs or investments. In risk analysis, probability factors are given to a range of estimated sales and costs so that the alternate outcomes can be calculated according to the probabilistic factors. The use of sensitivity analysis and risk analysis is probably best illustrated by the sort of questions asked of and answered by computer models.

For sensitivity analysis, the sort of questions to be asked include:

1. What effect would an increase in the price of raw materials have on net profits?
2. What would be the effects of changes in the selling prices?
3. If demand exceeds budget, could we meet the extra demand from budgeted resources?
4. What would be the minimum level of sales to make the project break even?

For risk analysis, the sort of questions to be asked include:

1. What is the probability of the 'most likely' level of return being attained for the project (i.e. 40%, 60% or even 100%)?
2. What would be the worst possible situation that could happen, and what is the probability of this happening?
3. What is the likelihood of the project attaining a return of X% (which could be the break-even point)?

Answers to these questions are practicable only by using computer models, not only because of the volume and complexity of the calculations involved but also because of the 'trial and error' approach that is involved. The facility of computer models to re-work calculations in a short time allows multiple changes to be made to input parameters, as we saw in Chapter 3.

A large volume of variables would necessarily result in a large volume of print-out which would be unmanageable in the normal course of appraisal. A method commonly used in risk analysis is to provide the results of simulation in graphic form. The illustration in Figure 5.11 is an example of how much information can be collated and presented by a computer on one page of print.

GRAPHICAL PRESENTATION

The example is based on actual work carried out by a computer model. The input data to the model included:

1. Four sales prices, each of which is estimated for a given volume of sales
2. Five forecast trends, any of which may be related to the level of sales volume selected from 1 above
3. Labour costs—standard cost rates for each machine required
4. Raw material costs—standard cost rate for each unit of production
5. Indirect costs—production overheads, sales and distribution costs and administration costs

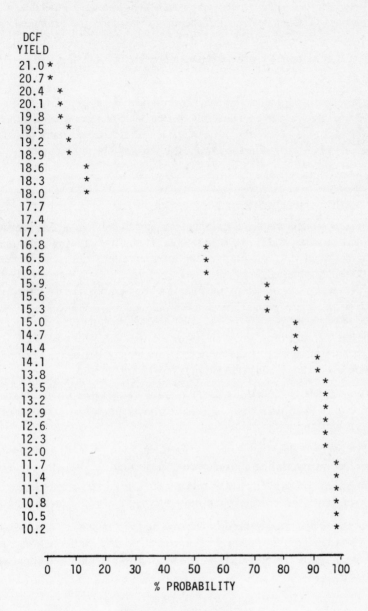

Figure 5.11   Risk Analysis

6. Plant and equipment costs (investment allowances are calculated), the number of machines required being governed by the estimated sales volume

7. The cost associated with setting up a new factory unit

8. Tax data

The resulting print-out in bar-chart form indicates for each level of return the probability in percentage terms of that level of return being attained. In the example given the probability of attaining the level of return expected was judged to be too low for the project to be attractive.

BUDGET FORECASTS

Computer models are being used increasingly to help managers determine business strategy and in the preparation of budgets, allowing experiments with ranges of data to discover the areas in which the most profitable results will be attained.

The system discussed in the following paragraphs is currently being used by a group with 13 separate trading companies selling a wide range of products.

It was found more convenient to divide the budget forecasting system into a number of individuals models for reasons of flexibility. The budget forecasting system is illustrated in Figure 5.12.

The number of models are divided into working models and consolidation models. The data used to calculate sales proceeds, gross margins, gross profits and trading profit included:

1. For each product: sales units, sales prices, cost of sales, fixed production costs and standard production cost per unit

2. For each company: transport and distribution costs, warehousing costs, selling costs, advertising and promotion costs and administration costs

Each cost is allocated to products according to its own basis of apportionment to calculate the trading profit for each product. In those companies where there was a wide variety of products, it was found more convenient to group the products by type.

TRADING SUMMARY STATEMENTS

The budget forecasting system produces five different statements, showing for each five years (the last full year's actual results, the actual results to date for the current year and the estimates for the remaining periods, the budgets for the next year, and forecasts for the following two years):

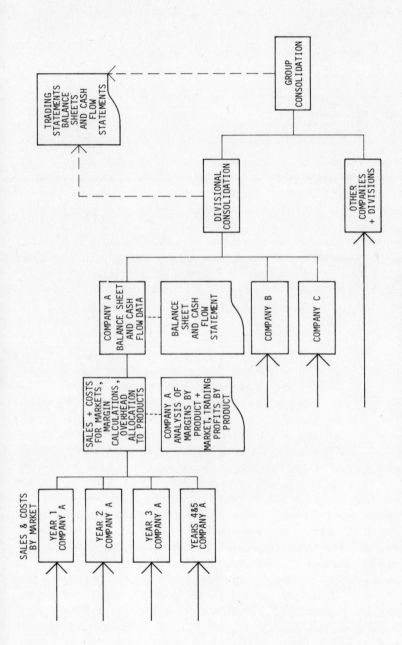

Figure 5.12 Budget Forecasting System

1. Sales, gross margins and trading profit by product for each company
2. Trading summary for each company and division, and for the group
3. Profit summary for each division and the group
4. Source and use of cash for each division and the group
5. Capital employed and net assets for each division and the group

One example of the trading summary statement for one of the companies is illustrated in Figure 5.13.

During the preparation of the budgets and forecasts, forecasts of sales volumes at various sales prices are tested by sensitivity analysis to arrive at the most satisfactory level of activity.

Draft budgets are reviewed at divisional and group level and usually require modification. The adjustments are re-input to the computer budget forecasting system and the budgets re-compiled. This sequence of events covers a period of several months before the budgets are finalised. The data for the next financial year is recorded on the computer's files for processing the budgetary control system discussed earlier in the chapter.

CONCLUSION

This chapter has illustrated how computers are being used to assist managers in their primary functions of planning and controlling. The development of computer-based financial planning and control systems has been dramatic over the past few years, and is likely to be just as dramatic over the next few years. This is not only because of the continuing rapid development of computer technology, particularly in systems for storing and retrieving data, in communications, in software and in the new data base management information systems, but also because managers are now having to respond much more quickly to changes in business policy caused by competitive and legislative forces beyond their control. Managers will, therefore, demand information systems that will provide them with up-to-date situations reports in the shortest possible time. This demand can be satisfied only by a computer.

Computers are, however, only the instruments by which control systems are made possible. A background of clearly defined business objectives, organisation structure and management responsibilities, and of precisely defined systems requirements and coding structures, are essential requirements for any effective control system. In addition there are also many questions that should be asked before embarking on sophisticated control systems, questions such as:

TRADING SUMMARY	SECOND DIVISION		A COMPANY LTD				STATEMENT No 2			
	YEAR 1 ACTUAL		YEAR 2 ESTIMATE		YEAR 3		YEAR 4		YEAR 5	
	£'000	%	£'000	%	£'000	%	£'000	%	£'000	%
1. Sales	4783	100.00	5483	100.00	7382	100.00	8594	100.00	9235	100.00
2. Gross margin	1223	25.57	1237	22.56	1961	26.56	2382	27.72	2538	27.48
3. Production	306	6.40	336	6.13	876	11.87	927	10.79	988	10.70
4. Gross profit	917	19.17	901	16.43	1085	14.70	1455	16.93	1550	16.78
5. Research and development	0	0.00	0	0.00	0	0.00	0	0.00	0	0.00
6. Transport	80	1.67	58	1.06	109	1.48	119	1.38	132	1.43
7. Warehousing	25	0.52	19	0.35	23	0.31	26	0.30	29	0.31
8. Profit before selling expenses	812	16.98	824	15.03	953	12.91	1310	15.24	1389	15.04
9. Selling expenses	119	2.49	121	2.21	129	1.75	140	1.63	151	1.64
10. Advertising and promotion	87	1.82	90	1.64	96	1.30	101	1.18	107	1.16
11. Profit before admin expenses	606	12.67	613	11.18	728	9.86	1069	12.44	1131	12.25
12. Administration expenses	164	3.43	175	3.19	184	2.49	198	2.30	213	2.31
13. Trading profit (after depreciation)	442	9.24	438	7.99	544	7.37	871	10.13	918	9.94
14. Yield of trading capital employed		58.74		35.80		42.02		59.54		58.75
15. Note: depreciation charged	48	1.00	58	1.06	58	0.79	59	0.69	59	0.64

Figure 5.13   Trading Summary Statement

1. In what ways will management effectiveness be increased?

2. Which management techniques are appropriate?

3. What will be the implications on management style?

4. What are the real information needs of managers?

5. What costs will be involved and does the value of the information to be provided justify these costs?

The answers to such questions will determine the type of system most appropriate to the particular business in terms of complexity and cost.

With the range of computer equipment available, from mini-computers upwards, and the variety of the facilities offered by computer bureaux, the modern manager has at his disposal a wider range of services than ever before for providing him with information that meets his requirements and at a cost that he can afford.

It is not out of place to conclude this chapter by quoting an extract, emphasising the importance of financial control information, from a book written by an accountant of an earlier era who lived more than 200 years before the first computer was installed. 'A tradesman's books are his repeating clock, which upon all occasions are to tell him how he goes on. If they are not duly posted, and if everything is not carefully entered in them . . . the tradesman is like a ship at sea, steered without a helm; he is all confusion, he can give no account of himself to himself, much less to anybody else; and is far from being qualified either to receive or make proposals in relation to marriage or any other considerable event in life' (Daniel Defoe, *The Complete English Tradesman*). The author of *Robinson Crusoe* in writing his essay on the accounting theory and practice of his time was as aware as the managing director of 1975 quoted earlier in the chapter of the vital need to be well informed at all times of the state of the business and the dangers of being 'all confusion'.

CHAPTER 6

Industrial Relations and Personnel Management

BY M. ST VINCENT

Punched cards were first used for analysing statistical data about people in 1889. It was then that Hollerith proposed the use of automatic processing equipment for analysing the results of the nation-wide census of the USA. When the use of his equipment was eventually extended into commercial and industrial environments it was again the processing of information relating to people that became a favourite application for accountants and data processing personnel alike. The degree of calculation involved, the repetitive nature of most of the processes and the volume of data to be manipulated made payrolls one of the earliest systems to be automated. Another important factor was the easy transference of payroll calculation techniques from one company to another and this was especially the case in the environment of a narrow-based but fast-growing technology where trained staff were at a premium.

When computers were initially introduced for commercial applications there was a tendency to bring them in firstly to 'replace' the punched card installations, and only secondly because of their potential for new data processing applications. It is not surprising therefore that payrolls were amongst the very early systems which were computerised. However, data processing was growing up and already a new breed of computer analysts and managers was emerging. They began to challenge the historical basis for selecting systems to be converted to computer processing and to question the validity of processing payrolls in the first place. In recent years, therefore, it has been less typical for new installations to start by handling the payroll first and now it is usual for feasibility studies to place more emphasis on the 'spin-off' benefits which emanate from computerised payrolls than upon the actual economics of the payroll calculation. It is in the areas of personnel information handling that the computer is beginning to make some highly valuable contributions to business and these will be examined later.

It must be emphasised that the starting point of the input to payroll systems varies considerably between companies since the means of recording raw data and determining extra payment amounts over and above basic rate also vary between companies. The one area common to all payrolls is the gross to net calculation whereby national insurance, graduated pension, company pension contributions, PAYE tax and other deductions are calculated and subtracted from the total earnings arrived at by adding basic pay, bonus (incentive) payments, overtime earnings and shift supplements.

Although deductions vary and different employees have different liabilities the gross to net calculation is so similar for big and small companies alike that a number of very competitive flexible payroll packages exist which perform this routine. Moreover, since this area is very susceptible to change at budget time, the use of a package supplied by a reputable software company does provide a degree of protection for the computer users: they no longer need to keep resources on one side for amending and keeping payrolls up to date. The packages usually provide basic accounting analyses as an integral part of the system and here, too, there is a degree of commonality in approach between most companies. It is usual for the cost of an employee to be allocated in proportion to the hours worked in any given department and a departmental account (or cost) code is used for classifying the information. A by-product of the system is often a record card produced whenever master file data is changed. This, kept by the wages office, carries historical data about each member of the payroll. These record cards are limited to data accumulated via the payroll system and, whilst useful reference documents on pay matters, are not suitable in themselves for replacing other personnel records. In the last ten years there has been growing interest in maintaining personnel records within a computer for a number of reasons:

a. Many larger companies now have well-developed job evaluation and grading schemes for both hourly paid employees and salaried staff. These schemes need to be monitored continually in order to ensure that the salary bands are not being abused and that the distribution of employees throughout the bands follows the intended pattern after taking into consideration factors such as age, time in job, service and similar criteria

b. Inflation appears to be a continuing and unavoidable evil and although we may be able to control the rate more effectively, even the most economically secure nations of the world seem unable to avoid it altogether. In such an environment companies need to review their payment structures more frequently and hence the administration of wage and salary changes across the board imposes unacceptable burdens on line management and personnel functions alike. Furthermore since a not infrequent weapon used by governments to hold down inflation is some form of statutory wage freeze or control, it is now becoming increasingly necessary to provide

Incomes Boards of one kind or another with statistical evidence of a company's compliance with the current regulations

c. More and more employees are now covered by company life insurances and pension schemes, both at the staff and at the shop floor levels. These schemes themselves require historical data, by employee, of service, wage/salary changes, age, pension contributions etc. in order that the company's liabilities and employees' benefits under the scheme can be calculated and evaluated

d. The move towards pay equality between the sexes has been accelerated by Government legislation in recent years and in order to ensure that progress is made realistically and smoothly towards compliance with this requirement it is again vital to obtain various analyses of salary by sex within job grade

e. The better planning of careers and succession routes and the measuring of 'performance in job' are now encouraging features of the personnel scene and consequently there is a need for classifying and recording the information emanating from appraisal interviews

When considering payrolls, reference was made to the calculation of bonus payments which vary considerably between companies. Whilst most standard payroll packages concentrate on the gross to net calculations, there is no doubt that the complexity of many incentive schemes is such as to make this a very labour-intensive area; consequently whenever the size of the payroll justifies it the computer is used for calculating bonus payments. This is an important factor in the highly volatile industrial relations scene of the 1970s since many companies are now revising or introducing bonus schemes as part of productivity deals and general wage negotiations. The monitoring of these schemes thus assumes greater importance and information relating to the breakdown of take-home pay by job and department is required by management on a regular basis.

The extension of the computer into all the above fields illustrates both the changing industrial relations climate within industry itself and the growing confidence being placed in the computer throughout business as an instrument of management.

DESIGN CONSIDERATIONS

It was not unreasonable for attempts to have been made to bring together the systems used for regularly paying employees and those used for recording historical information. However, because the basic objectives and timings of the two systems are different there is now a tendency to keep them separate for normal purposes but to link them, so that they share a single 'master' file of all employees' basic data, in order to prevent unnecessary duplication and to ensure the security and integrity of the data held.

Payrolls are of two basic types, those concerned with 'hourly paid' employees and those dealing with 'salaried' staff. The former type involves the multiplication of a basic hourly rate by the number of hours worked in order to determine the basic pay, whereas the latter normally takes a weekly rate, monthly rate divided by 4 or annual salary divided by 52 as the weekly earnings figure. It follows that the fully comprehensive hourly payroll systems differ in a number of respects from the salaried staff systems and they will therefore be considered separately.

HOURLY PAID PAYROLLS

An all-embracing system which incorporates incentive scheme calculations consists of the following input requirements per employee in addition to his home department code and clock number:

For each day worked the number of normal hours as shown on the clock card, the number of overtime hours and the details of which shift was worked if differential payments apply to the shifts. In addition a breakdown of the number of worked hours by the task or cost centre in which it was performed is also necessary. This data enables the calculation of basic hours, overtime hours (sometimes translated as a factor x basic hours) and shift supplements, and furthermore enables the allocation of the costs to the appropriate cost centres for analysis purposes.

Also required will be the accumulation of bonus scheme data either as it relates to the number of output units produced compared to the standard set by the industrial engineers or as it relates to the number of standard hours worth of work produced by the employee during the day. In either case the excess produced over standard qualifies for bonus payment and this is also required to be analysed by the cost centre.

The means of recording this daily data ranges from automatic clocking devices which incorporate badge reading and digital input features through to groups of clerks who add up the hours shown on each clock card and bonus ticket and summarise the data by employee either daily or weekly. A separate study of this very important area is essential when the computerisation of a payroll is being considered and there are a number of factors which need to be included in any such evaluation:

a. How many employees are involved in the payroll?

b. How many clerks are needed to summarise the data fully or partially?

c. How many clerks represent the absolute minimum (allowing for holidays etc.) who can staff the pay office adequately even assuming no calculations are necessary?

d. Are the rules relating to the qualification of basic, overtime and shift supplement hours straightforward and amenable to automatic operation?

e. How many incentive schemes are involved and do they all have a common pattern of calculation?

f. How time-critical is the payroll i.e. how long between the last day of accumulation of data and the day of payment?

g. What methods of transferring data from source to the computer centre are available?

h. Does weekly input of data impose severe peak load data preparation problems in the pay office and computer department, or can the peaks be fitted into lulls in the remaining work load?

There are other considerations, of course, and there are rarely simple answers to many of these questions. It is therefore not possible in a chapter such as this to recommend solutions; however a rigorous evaluation of at least these questions will throw up the most practical and economic solution for a particular set of circumstances. Suffice it to say that in the extreme case where clerks are used not only to summarise data weekly but also to calculate the bonus due per employee, it may still be sensible to use the computer for the gross to net and analysis roles.

Many companies who use packages for hourly paid payroll calculations start off by feeding summarised data into a gross-to-net system since this is easily handled by a standard package, and they subsequently develop programs of their own to handle the clerking duties and calculate bonus data so as to present this in the required format to the main common program. By adopting this route the standardisation of payroll calculation and analysis across a company can be achieved very easily without jeopardising local conditions in each of its plants or work centres. Furthermore, tailor-made systems can then be developed either on a plant by plant basis, or, if the company can meanwhile negotiate common schemes throughout, on a company-wide basis.

The use of a computer for the gross to net operation enables not only the accounting analyses to be produced but also labour statisitics on a plant by plant basis and these, in turn, can help management to determine the effect of different pay schemes, thus providing a range of more realistic alternatives when negotiating with the employees. Information detailing the breakdown of take-home pay by job category is now helping both management and unions to a better understanding of their mutual dependence or otherwise on such items as overtime. This understanding can only lead to better judgements relating to ideal manning levels i.e. is it better to build in some allowance in manning levels to help minimise overtime or is it better to pay overtime rates and run lean? The arguments in these types of evaluation are by no means as one-sided as might at first appear to be the case and reliable indisputable information is vital as an aid to good decision-making and improved industrial relations.

The daily data requirements have been referred to but there is also a need for certain standard data relating to each employee and cost centre such as hourly rates and bonus rates, tax code, gross pay to date, tax paid this year to date, graduated pension contributions to date, company pension scheme contributions, national insurance contributions and other routine deductions. This data is maintained on the payroll master file and all new starters need to be added to this file prior to the first payroll date after they join. Likewise any amendments to rates or standard data must be entered on the file in advance of the payroll run on which they become effective. A feature of payroll master files is that deletions from the file are normally forbidden except at the end of the tax year. This is because cumulative data relating to deductions for inland revenue purposes is required in order to produce P60 returns for all personnel employed by the company during the tax year. In fact it is feasible to extract information relating to leavers onto a separate file if the accumulation of ex-employee data becomes an embarrassment in terms of master file space; however this approach is rare.

One aspect of hourly paid payrolls is that in the United Kingdom they are usually produced weekly and usually result in the payment being made by cash. This brings with it three extra problems:

a. The security of the cash: not perhaps the DP man's immediate responsibility but a good analyst should nevertheless satisfy himself that this aspect is properly covered

b. The drawing of the correct currency denominations in order to make up the pay packets with the correct amounts. Here the computer can help in two ways, either by providing a detailed coin and note analysis or by rounding up or down the pay to the nearest convenient monetary unit. The remainder is then recorded on the master file and applied to the following week's pay calculation

c. The maintenance of deadlines, the DP manager's nightmare, concerns the day the hourly paid payrolls all fail to be processed and distributed on time and normal back-up procedures do not work! Employees who are paid weekly are naturally dependent on their wages arriving on schedule since their family budgets are geared around the weekly pay packet. Nothing is therefore as likely to cause industrial distrust and unrest as unreliable payroll performance. Later the question of back-up procedures will be considered in greater detail but this is clearly an area where both the analyst and the operations manager must be absolutely certain they have provided adequate cover

In the United States and on the Continent, companies often now produce fortnightly payrolls which, of course, halves the significance of the problems listed above. More important, they have also been more successful in persuading employees to accept payment through the cheque or credit transfer system with the consequent elimination of both the cash security and the cash analysis problems. British reticence in this respect is most unfortunate.

SALARY PAYROLLS

These can also be subdivided into those run each week and those run less frequently. For the reasons given relating to hourly paid payrolls there are incentives for companies to try to pay all staff by credit transfer on a monthly or four-weekly basis. In many cases the weekly salaries systems have now disappeared and all staff have accepted the longer payment cycle.

In order to persuade staff to change to monthly or four-weekly payment cycles most companies provide floats to employees during the transition period which are then repaid by deduction from subsequent payrolls. This is a worthwhile exercise since it simplifies the administration of the systems in addition to improving the security.

Salary payrolls are, generally speaking, much simpler to administer since incentive schemes are rare and payment during sickness is normal. In the latter case the program needs to handle adjustments resulting from employees claiming national sickness benefit since this amount must then be deducted from the next salary payment. Overtime and special payments are features of staff payrolls and are usually entered on special overtime input forms. It is not necessary to input other data for every employee on the staff on each occasion since the annual amount is held on the master file and the program calculates the sum to be paid for the period being covered.

An important aspect of salary master file input forms is that the employee's identity needs to be kept secret from the data preparation and control staff who are on the same payroll. To achieve this it is usual for a two-part record to be produced. The part of the record which provides fields for amending salary on the master file has space only for the employee's payroll number but does not contain the full name. Any identifying details, together with the variable data, are then submitted on a separate part of the records. For new starters both parts of the form are completed but sent separately to the computer department. For amendments to personal details or to salary only the appropriate portion of the record is completed and sent to the computer department. The positions of the employee's address and similar details on the form vary but usually are held on the salary portion of the document since they constitute a likely variable.

In other respects the gross to net system is common to the hourly paid systems and it is not unusual for a universal payroll package to be used for all employees in the company.

PERSONNEL RECORDS SYSTEMS

These systems began to be widely used in the late 1960s principally because the need to 'massage' data relating to grading schemes, salary bands and employees' appraisals became greater as more emphasis was placed on these features of personnel management. Another, more technical, reason was also a contributory factor, however. Whereas the 'hit rate' for payroll runs is exceptionally high (perhaps the highest in data processing) the 'hit rate' for many of the analyses required from personnel records could be quite low. Note that 'hit rate' is here defined as the number of record accesses per pass of the master file as a percentage of the total number of records. It follows that direct access facilities are really required for personnel records systems and these began to become financially more attractive in the late 1960s as disc files became cheaper and more reliable. The responsibility for personnel record systems usually rests with the personnel department, whereas payroll administration usually rests elsewhere and it is not uncommon for the master files in each case to be maintained quite independently, especially as their end use is different. Nevertheless this can result in a certain degree of data duplication and more recent developments attempt to provide a formal interface between the two systems. Where this formal link was not designed into the system there is a very real need to carry out periodic checks to ensure that the two files are in step. For staff systems, which tended to be the earlier ones, this is simplified by the practice of most companies of holding annual salary reviews for whole sections of the staff at one time. In this case the opportunity can be taken to use a turn round document from the personnel system for effecting the salary review and making the changes to the personnel system. An extract from this file is then used to update the payroll master file thus ensuring that at that point in time the files can be reconciled to each other. If the intermediate salary reviews and promotions are handled via the personnel system then an effective 'manual' interlock is provided between the two systems. The most important aspect of this interlock is that the personnel system always truly reflects the current situation and is not several weeks out of date. A personnel record system consists of the following basic elements:

1. Input validation program
2. Master file update program—including production of new record cards
3. Sundry regular analysis programs
4. Sundry *ad hoc* analysis programs

The first two programs are normally run once a week in order to ensure that the file is kept as current as possible. Many of the regular analysis programs constitute monthly or four-weekly requirements for monitoring staff movements within grades but some are linked to less frequent reviews such as the annual salary review already referred to above. Perhaps the major benefit of a personnel records system rests in the ability of personnel management to make *ad hoc* studies relating to the policies they administer. Whilst many of the programs required for this type of work are specified at the time the system is introduced, many of them represent one-off or very infrequent requests and are best handled by using a retrieval facility of some kind.

INPUT AND MASTER FILE UPDATING FOR PERSONNEL RECORDS SYSTEMS

The input documents for updating the file are of four basic types:

1. New employees
2. Record cards (amendments and leavers)
3. Turn round documents
4. Special purpose input documents

The input form for new employees contains basically the same information as the computer-produced employee's record card but is only used for establishing a new record on the master file. The record card on the other hand performs two functions, one being to provide a visible copy of the information on the file and the other to provide a facility for amending the file. This latter 'turn round' feature is particularly important since it helps to eliminate both clerical effort and a possible opportunity for transcription error. The record card therefore displays both the current information stored in the computer and space for manually entered amendment data. Leavers can be notified to the system by means of the record card which can be completed with coded details of the reason for leaving. As with payrolls, leavers are not removed entirely from the system and therefore this coded information can subsequently be used to study the reasons for leaving by department, location, job grade or any other category of interest to management.

It is not unusual for the reverse of both the new employee and the record card documents to be used for other purposes. For instance the reverse of a new employee form can be used to obtain authorisation for credit transfer payments and special deductions, and the reverse of the record card is normally used to record the recommendations and authorisation of changes by the employee's manager and the personnel department. An example of a typical personnel record card is shown in Figure 6.1. It is in three sections. As with payrolls, the facility exists for employee's name and salary details to be kept separate when the forms are submitted for processing. The upper portion of the three-section card is used as a permanent record in the initiating location if the other two sections are away for processing. This allows for plant or remote site personnel functions to send input documents to a central computer installation and still retain a basic record for quick reference and control purposes. The computer will, of course, produce a completely new and comprehensive record card after the amendment run with a new amendment number printed on the card. An important feature of a personnel records system is the need for amendment numbers to be controlled on a record-by-record basis as opposed to a file basis as for some other computer systems (*see* Figure 6.1).

Before considering the types of information that it is possible to obtain from a computer-based personnel system let us consider the other two forms of input. As mentioned earlier an important feature of the system is its ability to provide *turn-round tabulations* (in addition to the record cards) for helping to effect salary reviews etc. In this case it is possible to sort the records into 'department' and 'job duties within department' so that each manager can be given a comprehensive, logically structured list of his staff. The list can show most of the data held on the record, not least a history of salary movements, and will be set out in such a way that spaces are provided for completing the new salary change and new salary (as a cross-check). The layout needs to be such that by slicing the tabulation down the middle personal details of the employees (i.e. name) are segregated from the 'update' material such as employee number and salary. The use of 'data types' or codes to indicate to the computer program the type of amendment is common practice and these, of course, must also appear on the portion to be used for input.

The ease with which salary reviews for several thousand employees can be effected within very short time scales is in itself almost sufficient justification for the system. The 'across the company' salary review points are ideal for ensuring that both payroll and personnel master files are in step, even though regular direct links between the systems might not exist.

In addition to the three forms of input described it is also occasionally necessary to use other special input documents. This is to enable modification or addition to historical data held against a person on the file since the normal amendment mechanism simply changes information from its last held state to its new state. Because a valuable characteristic of the system is its ability to hold the history of jobs, grades and salaries by date for each employee, it may be necessary from time to time to correct errors in this historical data. Another very important extension of the system is for performance appraisals and although turn-round documents can be used to submit data for these, it is sometimes preferable to have special 'appraisal' input forms. The data submitted on these is invariably codified, both for compactness and for subsequent analysis and retrieval purposes. Unlike the annual salary review requirement the nature of appraisals is such that whilst this form of input results from an annual event per employee, the actual timing of appraisals is spread throughout the year and therefore a periodic file update is necessary.

ANALYSIS REPORTS—REGULAR AND *AD HOC*

So far the emphasis has been on maintaining an up-to-date master file and the hard copy personnel record. Apart from the desirability of uniform records throughout a company and the provision of an easy means to keep them up-to-date, the mechanics of maintaining the file are of less importance than the variety of end-use reports possible from a personnel system. These take two forms, those produced on a regular basis, and those produced as required by management.

Although the keeping of records relating to employees is normally the function of the personnel department there is always a need for departmental managers to have details of their own staff easily available. Without duplication of information and recording effort and the associated problems of reconciliation between the records, this objective is difficult to achieve manually. However, the computer system is able to provide lists of all staff by department, showing for each employee a synopsis of the information held on the master file. These lists can be further broken down into sub-categories, such as position on the organisation chart, job grading, sex, salary band, years of service etc. The method of handling some of these breakdowns will become evident later when coding structures are discussed. Certain listings of this kind are produced on a regular basis (i.e. quarterly, half-yearly) and these are normally the subject of special print routines which access the master file, sort the data and print to the prescribed format. Other varieties of output are normally produced on an as-needed basis; for these once-off purposes 'retrieval' programs are normally used and several proprietary software packages exist to help with the retrieval operation, although some companies write their own.

Staff Record   as at   amendment no.

IDENTITY NO.

SEX

TITLE

CHRISTIAN NAME/INITIALS

SURNAME

LOCATION

RATING

MAN./SUP.

I.O.M.

PART TIME

DATE OF ENGAGEMENT

WORKS

STAFF

DATE OF BIRTH

JOB TITLE

JOB DESC. CODE

NORMAL WKLY. HRS.

CURRENT SALARY

NAT. INS. NO.

ADDRESS

Staff Record   amendment copy

IDEN. NO.

EFFECTIVE DATE

SEX

TITLE

CHRISTIAN NAME/INITIALS (12)

SURNAME (25)

21

IDEN NO.

ADDRESS

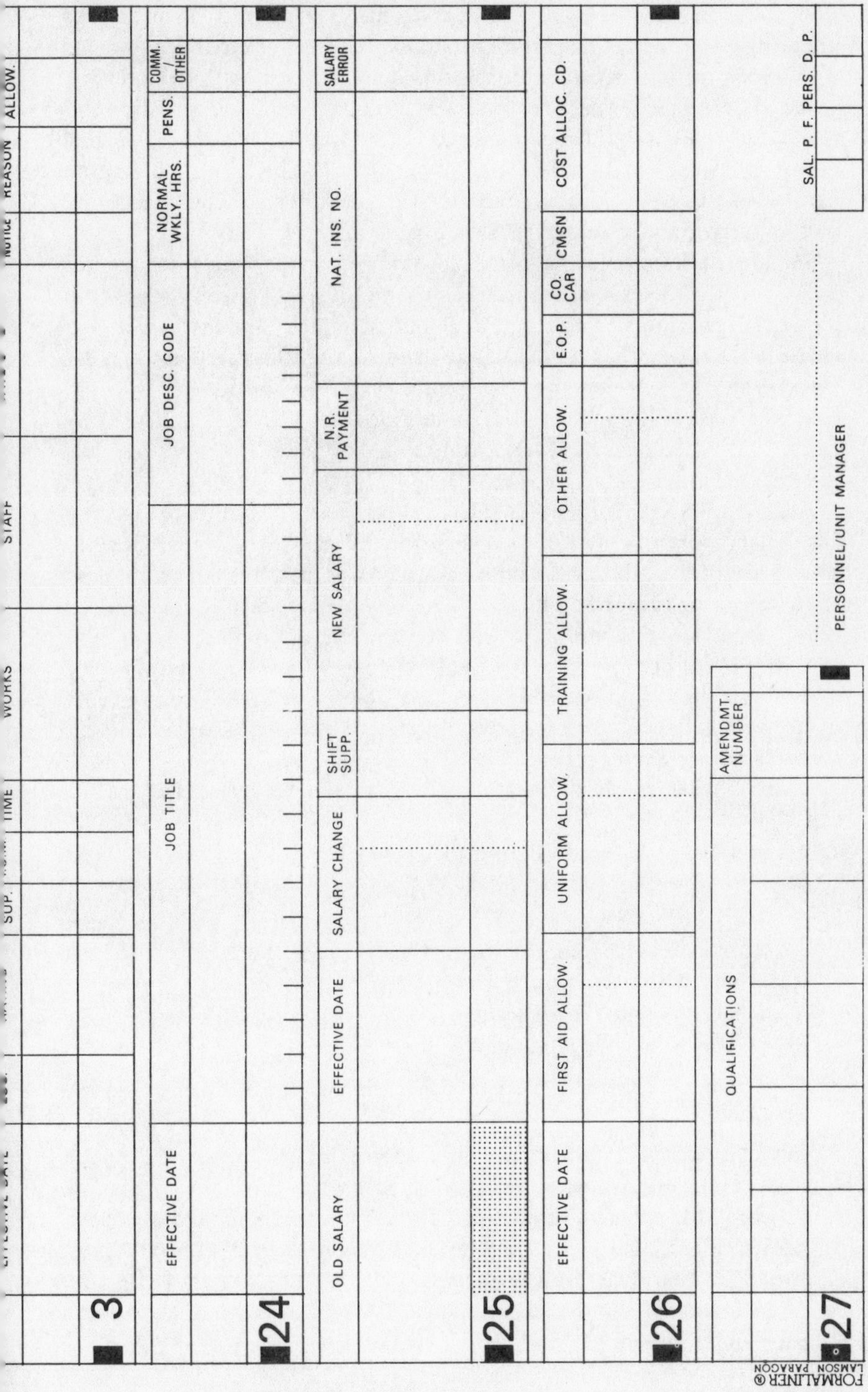

3
- EFFECTIVE DATE
- SUP.
- TIME
- WORKS
- STAFF
- REASON
- ALLOW.

24
- EFFECTIVE DATE
- JOB TITLE
- JOB DESC. CODE
- NORMAL WKLY. HRS.
- PENS.
- COMM. / OTHER

25
- OLD SALARY
- EFFECTIVE DATE
- SALARY CHANGE
- SHIFT SUPP.
- NEW SALARY
- N.R. PAYMENT
- NAT. INS. NO.
- SALARY ERROR

26
- EFFECTIVE DATE
- FIRST AID ALLOW.
- UNIFORM ALLOW.
- TRAINING ALLOW.
- OTHER ALLOW.
- E.O.P.
- CO. CAR
- CMSN
- COST ALLOC. CD.

27
- QUALIFICATIONS
- AMENDMT. NUMBER
- PERSONNEL/UNIT MANAGER
- SAL. P. F. PERS. D. P.

FORMALINER® LAMSON PARAGON

Figure 6.1

In order to help the personnel department to ensure that their policies are being consistently adhered to throughout all locations and departments it is important that regular (monthly/four-weekly) reports of salaries by grade are produced. These reports, which require special programs, show the range of actual salaries within the grade limits and the calculated mean compared to the mid point of the range. The display of output can be in the form of a scattergram or histogram or simply a listing of jobs in the grade in ascending (descending) order of salary.

Equally important to the personnel function is the ability to monitor salary movements on a regular basis and this too usually gives rise to special programs. These result in output which shows the size and incidence of salary changes during the period being considered and enables the changes to be monitored to ensure that they fall in line with: (i) company policy; (ii) industrial/commercial salary trends as indicated by current advertisements; (iii) Government policy; and (iv) voluntary pay rise restraint criteria.

Many sizable companies even today do not have well-structured grading and salary schemes and this was particularly evident when Government legislation affecting incomes policies was first introduced. Those firms operating properly designed and monitored schemes were much better placed in relation both to the Government authorities and to their own employees because they were able to demonstrate that logical salary scales were in operation and were also able to show which elements of normal pay rises were covered by genuine merit awards and which elements were to keep pace with the cost of living.

Other typical regular reports required by the personnel and salary departments include:

1. *Leavers List:* all leavers during the period being considered are listed showing reason for leaving

2. *Birthday List:* a list of employees who have reached a point at which a salary increase is due (juniors/trainees) or, at the other end of the spectrum, are due to retire

3. *Alphabetic Synopsis List:* by location and/or department which may meet some of the needs described earlier

4. *Staff Indices:* listing all staff in either alphabetic or identity number sequence

5. *Pensions Analyses:* listing employees approaching retirement during the next period and showing details of their employment history so that provision for payment of pension can be made. Also an analysis of the company's liabilities to its employees as required both in general and specific cases. This feature is particularly useful for managing the pension scheme and the pensions manager is often amongst the earliest users of the system

6. *Careers Progression Lists:* as specified by parameters which can be set up by the personnel staff development manager. These lists, together with 'progression now' lists, provide the manager with information regarding those employees who are ready for promotion as assessed during the annual appraisal. The reports indicate such information as current job description, time in present job, job history, qualifications, present grade and salary, and coded information regarding the appraiser's recommendations for promotion. The coded data covers such considerations as whether the employee is suitable for promotion outside his or her current department or whether the promotion potential is within the current department. Also some indication of time span is usually given such as suitable immediately, within one year, within two years etc.

The use of a computer to help in career planning is a relatively recent feature in the United Kingdom and has arisen principally from the introduction of more scientific methods in the personnel and industrial relations functions.

Local authorities, the nationalised industries and the civil and military services with their large payrolls and very formal structures were early leaders in the use of computers in the personnel and payroll fields, but did not link in appraisal and career planning facilities as early as some of the firms in the private sector.

The concept of career scheduling is shrouded by many emotional overtones especially on the part of the employees themselves, and to the extent that the computer system can demonstrate an unbiased and logical method of highlighting promotion candidates many of the anxieties can be removed. Ultimately the system does rely on the judgement of the employee's manager and *his* manager in turn, since they are responsible for the appraisal assessment which is fed into the system, but at least both manager and employee are absolutely clear about their respective roles and the employee knows that his name will not be overlooked. The employee, too, is able to express his career wishes during the appraisal and these are taken into consideration by the manager and personnel department when completing their own assessment of performance.

It will have been seen that there are a large number of different types of report available to management once the record system has become established. The regular reports discussed above are all used for monitoring or planning particular aspects of personnel management but are by no means the limit of the information which can be acquired from the system. In practice a major benefit of the system is its ability to produce *ad hoc* reports either using versions of the regular programs or else using a retrieval package. The *ad hoc* requirements stem from a variety of needs both in the line and personnel management areas but perhaps the most impressive are those used in determining new personnel policies and often instigated by the managing director or board of the company.

PENSIONS SYSTEMS

So far the systems considered have been concerned with the maintenance and analysis of records relating to staff currently employed by the company. However, staff who have left the company usually continue to represent a liability to the company in terms of its pension and insurance schemes. Many leavers do not immediately become eligible for pension insurance payments since they have simply changed jobs. These constitute 'withdrawals' from the ongoing day-to-day running of the pension system but remain in a frozen state until one day they or their next of kin become beneficiaries under the pension scheme. However, many of the leavers result immediately in the pension and insurance benefits becoming active. Thus the pension is due either to the employee or to his next of kin. The mechanism for actually making the payments is usually an extension of the normal staff payroll system; however there is also a need to maintain separate records of pensioners, widows/orphans and withdrawals as distinct from the 'actives' i.e. those employees still working for the company and adding to their benefit. It is therefore necessary to develop a sub-file of the personnel record system which holds details of the accrued benefit due to ex-employees of the company and such information as the next of kin or benefactors nominated by the employee.

The reason for keeping details of withdrawals (leavers) in the same system is not only that there are common information requirements between these and pensioners and widows but also that there is a dynamic fluidity between the groups. The withdrawal of today becomes the pensioner of tomorrow or gives rise to the widow the day after!

Although some of the information required by the pensions system is similar to that held on the personnel records system there is also a good deal of extra data that is required. This is particularly true in relation to the composition of the pension commitment for the member and his widow/orphan. The existence of the system enables the pensions department to carry out analytical work on the pension funds employed by the company and to monitor the company's commitment in this field. An example of a typical pensions record card is shown in Figure 6.2.

INTEGRATING THE SYSTEMS

At the outset to this chapter it was explained that because the time cycles and processing requirements of payrolls and personnel records are different there has been a tendency to keep the basic systems independent but

PENSION DATA CARD

as at / /

RECORD FOR

Computer Ref. No   Record Code   Card No   DD Indicator

Identity No   Minutes   BUPA   o/s Debts   Personal Policy   Total Pension Amount

Payment Address (if different from Member's)

FUND MEMBER

Member   Sex   Born   Normal Retirement Date   Actual Retirement Date   Location

Fund No   Annuity No   Nat. Ins. No   Pension Code   / /   / /   (Staff)   / /

Address   Date of Engagement (Works)   / /   (Staff)   / /   Date Deceased

Pens. Service (Works)   yrs   mths   (Staff)   yrs   mths   / /

MEMBER / PENSION POSITION

Ref No	Payment Area	Type	Paid to	Chge- able	Notes	Amount Per Annum	Date Paid up	Date Commenced	Pen. Pay Freq
01									
02									
03									
04									
05									
06									
07									
08									
09									
10									
11									
12									
13									
14									
15									
16									

Sickness Scheme   Pension Code   Sex   Born

WIDOW OR ORPHAN

Ref No	Payment Area	Type	Paid to	Chge- able	Notes	Amount Per Annum	Date Paid up	Date Commenced	Pen. Pay Freq
01									
02									
03									
04									
05									
06									
07									
08									
09									
10									
11									
12									
13									
14									
15									
16									

Supp. Grant   Termination Date / /   Pension Guarantee

Death Benefits (1) £   (2) £   Code   (3)   Identity No   Born / /   Age Admitted   Sex

Commuted Pension   AVC (1)   (2)   Name   Date Deceased / /

Disability Benefit   From / /   To / /   Relationship to Member

BENEFIT NOMINEES

(1) Name   Sex   Relationship to Member   Notes

Address

(2) Name   Sex   Relationship to Member   Notes

Address

PAID UP POLICY HOLDER / WITHDRAWAL

Min No   Insurance Co (1)   EPB   (2)   Employees Conts Paid   Employees Retained Conts   Total   Towards EPB   Contracted Out period   From   To / /

Type   Retained Conts   Tax Payable   Net Refund   Tax   Dedn. for PIL   Reason for leaving   Age Admitted

Employee Transfer Payment   Total Transfer Payment   New Employer   Date Leaving / /

Figure 6.2

provide a linkage mechanism, by means of a computer file, at certain times of the year. An added reason for this approach is that historically the systems have evolved at different times and as experience and confidence are gained, extensions and further requirements are conceived. Also the early records systems tended to deal with staff employees where reconciliation between the systems is less of a problem.

There is a growing tendency to develop parallel systems for hourly paid employees, especially now that companies are undertaking wider obligations to meet new pension requirements—such as the introduction of earnings related schemes for hourly paid workers. Recent advances in creating and operating data bases and in the media for file storage have meant that new design considerations come into play. No longer is there a tendency to set up three separate systems with only tentative links between them and with the corresponding duplication of input requirements. Instead systems are now being developed which, whilst retaining the integrity of the different files for processing and analytical purposes, do nevertheless integrate the data flows between the systems.

It is feasible to integrate 'package' payrolls into such a system and an overview of one approach to the problem is shown in Figure 6.3. It will be seen that new starters are initially established on the payroll master file in order to ensure payment on the first payroll day after joining. However an extract of the 'common data' is then used to establish a basic record on the pension/personnel master file. Ideally the addition of payroll data to this master file coincides with the arrival of other personnel data not required for the payroll. If it does not, then the transfer of data from the payroll file automatically generates new-start input reminder documents for adding the extra data required by the personnel/pensions system, and these are then fed in during the following week in order to update the main personnel/pensions record file. Following this update an employee's record card is produced for use by the local personnel department. It should be noted here that there can be three possible sources of data for the integrated system—the wages/salary administration function at the office or plant location, the local personnel function and the central pensions department. This is one reason why separate input documents may be required for payroll, personnel and pensions data.

The complete system can provide all of the types of information discussed earlier in the chapter as well as provide actuarial valuations for both current members, pensioners, deaths and withdrawals. An added feature resulting from the use of a data base type of file structure is that on-line enquiry facilities can be provided for the pensions office in order that quick evaluations of pensions due can be obtained. This facility can be extended to provide on-line enquiry facilities for personnel managers at all locations.

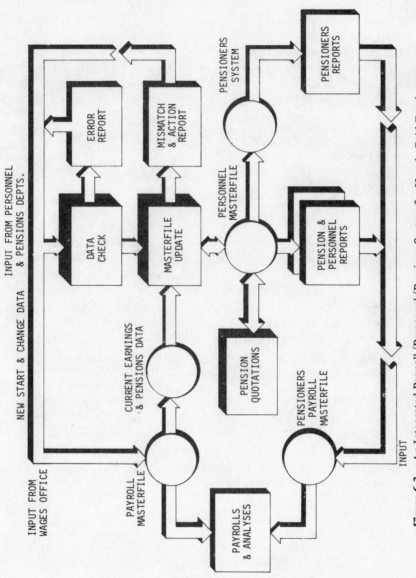

Figure 6.3   An Integrated Payroll / Personnel / Pensions System for Hourly Paid Employees

When employees become pensioners then their details are extracted by the computer from the personnel records file and set up on a separate pensioners file. It will be seen therefore that such a system has all the elements of the three separate systems discussed earlier but that now data is entered only once and is retained and transferred within the total system. This is an important factor when dealing with hourly paid schemes since these tend to be more volatile as well as larger in size than staff systems. However the technique employed for hourly paid can clearly be used for staff and new systems designs will be inclined to this more integrated approach.

TECHNIQUES EMPLOYED IN PAYROLL/PERSONNEL SYSTEMS

CODES

Reference has been made earlier to the use of codes for submitting and holding data in these systems and it is worth considering the different types of code needed in more detail. The reason for using codes is twofold, they are shorter than more descriptive data and also are easier to use for manipulating data, in sorting, collating etc. Because codes are not always easily translated by managers who have access to computer outputs, it is usual to hold a translation table in the computer to ensure that information on the reports is clearly understood.

Some of the fields maintained in coded form are: Employee number (Clock no./Identity no.), Location code (which plant or office), Sex, Rating/grade, Reason for leaving, Job title, Pension type, Cost allocation/ work centre, Job titles to which promotable, Appraiser's identity no., Appraiser's manager's identity no. and Qualifications code. One or two of these codes will also be used by other systems within the company and typical examples of these are the location code and the cost allocation/ work centre codes. Others are very simple and consist of one digit or letter e.g. Sex (M or F). It is not intended therefore to describe all of these in detail; however, some do have distinctive features which need elaboration.

The type of code used for identity number is common to the employee, his appraiser and the appraiser's manager. The size of this code depends on the total number of employees in the system. It is, of course, the main linkage between all the systems discussed and constitutes the minimum data that has to be duplicated. The code is usually issued on a random basis, i.e. not strict alphabetical sequence, in order to make it impossible for the casual observer to identify the person from the code alone. It is not usual to build dual features into this code (i.e. use it for location identity purposes) since once issued, the code stays with the employee for all time and remains static irrespective of the changes in location, job titles etc. *Codes are never reissued to other employees* because of the need to maintain the integrity of the employee's data throughout his working life, retired life, and his designated beneficiary's life. It follows that the code size and sequence need to cater for considerable expansion so that for 10,000 'active' employees the code might be seven digits in size, giving a maximum of nearly ten million employee numbers.

The rating or grading code consists of two parts, first a single-digit indicator of the staff category in which the employee falls and second a simple alpha/numeric code of the position within the category, the size of the secondary code being determined by the number of grade positions.

The job title code is usually structured so as to position the job within the hierarchical system of the department, division and company. An example of such a code is given below:

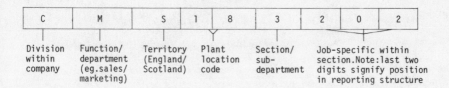

| C | M | S | 1 | 8 | 3 | 2 | 0 | 2 |

Division within company | Function/ department (eg.sales/ marketing) | Territory (England/ Scotland) | Plant location code | Section/ sub- department | Job-specific within section.Note:last two digits signify position in reporting structure

It will be seen that by analysing data using the job title code it is possible to produce an organisation chart by computer and this is a useful by-product from the personnel system for keeping the organisation details up to date. Certain fields of this full job title code (e.g. function and specific job codes) are used when entering appraisal data to the system. Three sets of career progression data are submitted, a list of job positions to which the employee may be promoted, together with the number of years before he is ready, a list of sideways-move jobs and 'when-ready' indicators, and a list of jobs to which the employee aspires. In each case the function and job codes are used to indicate the type of job to which the employee could be moved. When a vacancy arises in one of these jobs then a selection of all employees who are promotable/movable to the position can be made by searching the file for the appropriate job code.

The reason-for-leaving code is used to determine trends in the pattern of leaving as well as to record for future reference why an employee left. Normally a single alphabetic character or two numeric digit code is sufficient for this purpose. The allocation of the code can be grouped into three categories 'discharged by the company', 'resignation by the employee' and 'general' (e.g. retirement, death etc.).

INFORMATION RETRIEVAL METHODS

Most of the commercial payroll packages provide limited information retrieval facilities. These are designed to access the payroll files and produce many of the more standardised requirements such as bank lists and cost analyses; however, some of the other *ad hoc* needs can also be satisfied using these systems. As with other retrieval systems they make use of parameters for specifying the selection rules and print formats but usually only provide limited calculation capabilities such as addition and subtraction.

In order to obtain more powerful retrieval facilities many companies have developed a generalised parameter driven package of their own or else have obtained such a package from a commercial software house. These packages normally provide for the retrieval and merging of information from more than one file and also allow more complex calculations to be carried out. Thus they can be used to extract and compare data from both the payroll and personnel records files if desired.

ON-LINE FACILITIES

There are five basic ways in which on-line facilities can be associated with payroll and personnel systems:

a. On-line entry of data in batch mode
b. On-line entry of data in transaction mode
c. On-line enquiry of information from one record
d. On-line enquiry and analysis of information from several records
e. Use of on-line time-sharing for modelling alternative strategies

The degree to which any of these methods is appropriate will vary with the needs and size of the individual company but some general rules can be applied even though they are not exclusive.

On-line batch entry of data is most appropriate for submitting input to payroll runs where large quantities of data need to be prepared for input, transmitted and submitted to the computer within a limited time. Either the data can be recorded on disc or tape at the centre to await other input data from elsewhere before the processing run is activated by the control operators, or the processing run can be instigated by the remote location. The former method is most common where a number of locations can be streamed together for economy of processing purposes.

On-line transaction entry can be used to update master files and provides a good method of keeping the personnel and pensions files current. Clearly a coded 'lock' must be programmed into the update programs to prevent access except by authorised members of the personnel department. Few systems yet use this method of amending the master file but it is likely to gain favour as more and more on-line hardware and software facilities become available.

The third and fourth ways of using on-line capabilities are in the short term the most rewarding since they allow selected staff in the personnel department to determine the status of individual records, in reply to enquiries by management and/or the employee, as well as to carry out many of the *ad hoc* analyses referred to earlier. An important advantage of using this method of retrieving information is that it obviates the need for many of the hard copy records kept by management and also is an aid to security.

Most small or medium-sized computer installations are unable to afford *time-sharing* on a regular basis; however there are a number of bureaux who offer attractive time-sharing services. Although 'what if' simulations in the personnel field can be carried out by means of a series of batch runs using the systems already described, for ease of use it is often better to run these simulations in time-sharing mode. Typical applications include the analysis of alternative proposals in advance of and during wage negotiations; the analysis of alternative manning level versus overtime strategies; the structuring of a career development versus qualification by discipline model to investigate the type and mixture of new graduate recruits necessary to ensure a stable succession hierarchy.

This use of the computer as both a tactical and a strategic planning tool is becoming prevalent in all areas of activity e.g. finance, sales/marketing, production planning and so on. However, the personnel departments are amongst the forerunners in using a computer in this way and a great deal of exciting work is now being done in this area.

SECURITY

Throughout this chapter reference has been made from time to time to the need for security in one form or another and this is very important in respect of both personnel records and the payroll. There are several different facets to be considered:

a. *Physical Security:* The protection of the computer-held records and programs against damage, both malicious and accidental, and against machine failure. Also the provision of good recovery procedures

b. *Security against Fraud:* The protection of the systems and data against their fraudulent manipulation to benefit an individual or a group of individuals

c. *Security against Industrial Dispute:* This is particularly relevant to hourly paid payrolls and their critical deadlines. These can be jeopardised by a dispute occurring at any one of the several links in the data processing chain

d. *Privacy of Data held on files:* Even where published grading schemes are in force the actual salary/wage of an individual employee is seldom for general publication and there is a very real need to ensure that only the employee and certain designated staff have access to this information. Likewise there are many personal details relating to an employee which need to be safeguarded, not least being the data resulting from appraisals

PHYSICAL SECURITY

This is covered by the general security plan for the installation and, together with security against industrial dispute, can best be safeguarded by ensuring that good, well-rehearsed back-up procedures exist and that a proper 'duplicate copy' system is practised for all key files. It is normal for grandfather, father and son files to be retained so that recovery can go back two generations if need be. At least one of these generations should have a duplicate copy held at a secure remote site together with a security copy of the program. In addition to the files it is also necessary that the data fed in on each of the update runs is kept for the three generations mentioned. Where a file is part of a data base system either the whole system can be 'dumped' or else the file itself selected for back-up. In addition to the back-up files and data, it is vital that well specified and documented recovery procedures exist and these must cover the processing of the payroll on alternative installations in case a major equipment breakdown occurs. In the case of industrial disputes within the post office, railways etc. which might jeopardise the transfer of data or output, there are usually alternative methods of transport which can be used and again these should be specified in the procedures prepared for the computer centre.

FRAUD

Fraud can be effected in a number of ways, the most obvious of which are:

1. Addition of fictitious employees to the files
2. Submission of data relating to an employee such as to make his reimbursement larger than is due
3. Manipulation of the programs themselves

The principal protection against both (1) and (2) is to limit the source of amendments to the files and data to the personnel and/or payroll offices. In both cases it is expected that these staff are trustworthy but in any case regular checks by the company's auditors are normally sufficient to ensure their honesty. For this reason good, well-documented audit trails need to be built into the system and agreed with the auditors before the system goes live. Where terminals are used for submitting data this method of control can be strengthened by the use of personalised passwords which only allow specified staff to amend the master files. Where terminals are not used then the risk is extended to the data control and preparation area but batch controls on crucial data such as the money and hours worked enable the payroll/personnel staff to check the integrity of the input. (*Note*—Under this system, for an employee to increase his pay he must first reduce that due to someone else and that change is unlikely to go unnoticed for long!) The regular listings of the personnel master file which are made available to management provide an opportunity for checking the financial data held against each employee.

The third potential area for fraud is more difficult to monitor and again a high degree of trust is necessary with respect to the analysts and programmers responsible for the system. However it would often need all members of the team to be party to the fraud for it to be successful and independent spot checks on the program listings can provide some disincentive to the casual rogue. One way of avoiding the problem altogether is to use a standard package from an independent software house, in which case access to the programs by the installation staff is not necessary except for the inclusion of changes submitted by the suppliers.

PRIVACY OF DATA

Data held on the files can be controlled in a number of ways. Where magnetic tapes are used for main file storage purposes these can be held in safes or cabinets or even chained and padlocked in their racks. The key to the safes etc. can then be retained by the personnel or payroll department and only made available for authorised runs under the supervision of a responsible member of that department. This then ensures that these files are not accessed nor information retrieved without the permission of the authorised department. As a further check a copy of the computer log during the time the files are on the machine can be taken and kept with the file as evidence that access via the console or illegal programs has not occurred.

However, when data base files are used it is likely that either the files are on-line for considerable periods or else they share a disc file with data for other systems. In this case physical control is more difficult and coded protection of the files becomes more important. In the on-line situation this can be effected by means of a designated terminal located in the personnel or payroll office. This terminal can then have its own sign-on code and furthermore access can be limited to specific personnel, who must key in their own individual coded password.

One important point to stress, however, is that none of the measures mentioned can be guaranteed proof against the determined law breaker or a major disaster. All of them are aimed at limiting casual infringement by otherwise normal, well-balanced employees and at providing protection against normal hazards.

CONCLUSION

The need for accurate information relating to the industrial relations scene was never greater than now. Managers need to understand a great deal more about the effects of pursuing particular personnel policies and equally require speedy performance measurements to help them monitor the schemes they introduce. Employees are increasingly finding themselves part of large amorphous organisations as more and more companies merge or become nationalised. As a result they fear that their talents and needs will be overlooked by hardpressed management struggling to keep up with the paperwork.

The use of computers to produce management control information in varying forms is conventional so that their extension into the field of personnel management is not surprising. However, what is ironic is that the impersonal computer is helping to persuade employees that they are not viewed as another number on the payroll but are recognised as people with the human needs for job satisfaction and fair play and with personal qualities such as experience, qualifications and long service. The use of computers in the personnel field is thus of growing importance and its full potential is only now beginning to be realised; it might be expected, therefore, that the extension of this use will be rapid and extremely fruitful.

CHAPTER 7

Managing the Customer

By B. Doouss

With the evolution of business practice there has been considerable change in both the methods of selling and the systems employed by both the supplier and the customer. Growth in size and complexity have occurred in the normal evolution for added efficiency in both areas. This has affected the administrative and physical systems, the products and the terms of trade.

Customers are becoming increasingly sophisticated as they themselves join buying groups or become integrated within larger organisations. The understanding of profitability has improved and the techniques of selling have become very much more skilled, requiring additional information to be able to make effective use of the new system. Along with this have come changes in the structure of delivery, associated with warehouse and selling systems and also terms of trade and invoicing methods appropriate to these new situations. With greater understanding of market segmentation, the number of products and the packs in which they are sold have proliferated considerably, giving many new problems in selling and stock inventory control. A greater need for both supplier and customer to get together for mutual profitability has been recognised with discount payments being increasingly 'earned' rather than given as a straight percentage. With the increased awareness of marketing techniques there are new developments in trade terms and in the variety and type of promotional activity. This new awareness has largely made manual invoicing and stock systems very cumbersome to operate and often unsuitable for giving the necessary information required for selling and marketing activity. The development of 'consumerism' also brings the need to be much more consistent in overall policies and could even develop on similar lines to the Fair Trading Acts in the USA.

TRADE TERMS

Trade terms which positively help the supplier and yet give satisfactory discounts to the customer will be developed in the next few years. They are: quantity terms, performance/growth discounts, co-operation/partnership discounts, prompt settlement/cash discounts or interest charged on outstanding accounts, other special purpose discounts, temporary price reductions and bonuses related to promotional discounts.

QUANTITY TERMS

Quantity terms can be used to reduce costs in two areas:

a. By stimulating larger orders of individual products to reduce handling in the warehouse

b. By encouraging larger total orders to reduce the number of times that delivery is required

The former is encouraged by special prices for whole cases, layers or complete pallets of individual products. The latter is encouraged by special discounts related to total size of order; for instance, total number of cases, pallets or even complete rail-car or truck-loads.

The terms need to be realistic in representing the savings to the supplier and will often result in different ways of handling deliveries by the customer, such as delivery to a central warehouse for a chain of outlets instead of individual delivery to each selling point. From a supplier's point of view the greater the quantity of direct delivery from the source of production, rather than passing through intermediate warehousing facilities, the greater the significance of the savings obtained. The advantage of computer systems is that a very complex price list can be completely handled by the logic of a computer. Attractive terms given in this way may induce the customer to buy all his goods from a single supplier to attract the best quantity terms. Having correctly applied the terms, the analysis of their performance is a normal by-product of the invoicing process.

PERFORMANCE/GROWTH DISCOUNTS

These are generally arranged to reward the customer for exceptional growth of sales related to a particular supplier's products. They may be measured in three ways:

1. By level of turnover in either financial or tonnage terms. (In a time of considerable inflation tonnage or quantity is often a better guide than turnover figures)

2. By means of a negotiated specific target for a given time period for a named customer, either based on individual outlets or total company performance

3. By percentage of achievement above target

These special discounts can be arranged in different ways as a total discount on all business if the target is reached, or a discount on all sales above the target. Such discounts are usually given retrospectively after the performance reference period has been completed.

CO-OPERATION/PARTNERSHIP DISCOUNTS

The two previous discounts have been awarded for the size of order or general overall performance. It is also possible to agree on specific activities that will be carried out by the customer for which a special discount will be given. Samples of these are (i) area of display or special display area; (ii) overall stock levels; (iii) number of products stocked; and (iv) special selling activity.

Results of this type of agreement can be monitored by suitably designed computer systems.

PROMPT SETTLEMENT

It is becoming increasingly common to offer discounts to encourage customers to pay within given periods or to charge interest on overdue accounts or to insist on deposits from late payers. The principle of charging interest on overdue accounts has been established by the Access and Barclaycard type of systems.

SPECIAL PURPOSE DISCOUNTS AND INCENTIVES

These can be applied to encourage a certain regular rate of order or specific large orders which help to clear a particular surplus of a slow-moving item. In addition to this, special prizes can be given to individual agents or customers for particular agreed target sales within a specific time period.

TEMPORARY PRICE REDUCTIONS AND PROMOTIONS

These are generally either a special price for a fixed period or for a fixed quantity. They are used to promote sales during time periods where the market is slack and production facilities are therefore under-used or to promote an item of which there is more than adequate stock, to create a continuing customer demand or to reduce stock of a particular item. They can also be applied on the principle of the 'baker's dozen' where a unit is given away free with a specified quantity purchased. A computerised system ensures standard application and the opportunity to analyse results.

BONUS

This is a tactical tool applied to a specific order to encourage the customer to increase the quantity of selected promoted products or to extend the range of products ordered. Usually bonus takes the form of a deduction from the invoice total.

'Bonusing' is commonly used as a trade promotion in conjunction with other marketing activity directed at the consumer to launch a new product or to increase the market penetration of an existing product.

The general principles of discount by 'performance' will certainly be applied more in the future. This is all part of the changing customer scene with more realistic and appropriate means of interesting the customer, resulting in mutually more profitable business. ·

INFLUENCING THE CUSTOMER

A major question is: 'What "tools" can be provided for management and the selling agents, with which they can influence the customer into increasing profit for himself and the supplier?' New 'tools' are required to manage the *total* sale in terms of profitability rather than using turnover or quantity as the only yardstick. All this means developing a system which can readily demonstrate account profitability.

The major areas for study when we are trying to influence the customers are: obtaining an order and, having obtained it, increasing its size; ensuring that there is a profitable 'mix' of products, and giving appropriate customer service in delivery frequency, trade terms and credit, using appropriate methods and costs of selling. These will be examined to show how computerised information can help focus attention on defined target areas. Confusion usually arises where there are many customers on whom there is a large amount of different information available, such as packs sold, methods of service, terms of trade and credit. Any manual system fails to give the appropriate information from which the maximum profit from each customer can be obtained. Generally, systems which deal with the customer have been developed piecemeal and the true advantages of computerised systems have never been realised.

This establishes the first principle: that a total system for the customer should be designed so that, as shown later in the chapter, the inter-relationship between the order, the cost of obtaining it and the profit therefrom is known. The major influences on the order, its size and profitability are clearly demonstrable, but the area of customer service is an issue of balance in that additional customer services, such as special selling means or additional delivery frequency, are extra costs which have to be matched against the profit accruing from additional sales. It is this kind of influence on each customer which has to be closely watched.

It is interesting to compare the various methods of obtaining an order— post, telephone and personal call—and their relative costs.

POST

Orders can be received by post, individual letter or on a company order form in relation to mailed or advertised information on items or products for sale. This method is slow and gives little inducement to the customer to purchase greater quantities or in a manner which maximises profit. In many instances, where there are a large number of customers with small purchases, it may be the only method which can be afforded. The post is used by the mail order houses but even they are using noticeably more agents.

TELEPHONE

Use of the telephone can be in two areas:

1. Receiving orders initiated by the customer in response to advertising or previous information (such as a catalogue)
2. Deliberate telephone selling, which is successful particularly for repeat items, whether in consumables or durables

PERSONAL CALL

Personal calls can be made by a variety of persons. Varying costs are incurred in making the sales. Calls may be made by:

  a. A representative, using a company car, who pre-books orders
  b. A part-time sales force of housewives or moonlighters
  c. A salesman with the goods (van sales)

The form of selling chosen clearly depends on the type of product to be sold and the expertise required by the salesman in obtaining an order from a customer. A full representative is obviously necessary in the more technical area, but the other methods are successful where the knowledge and skills required to complete a sale are relatively limited, such as in consumer items. A fuller discussion on the way the computer can help in judging the effectiveness of different sales contacts is given later in the chapter.

THE TOTAL CUSTOMER SYSTEM

It is now appropriate to consider the total system resulting from taking an order and supporting the overall selling and management activity.

The customer base can be many thousands, and a very large product and pack range can be sold to any of them. It is, therefore, necessary to examine the structure of information and the means of creating a more profitable business as a result of it (*see* Figure 7.1).

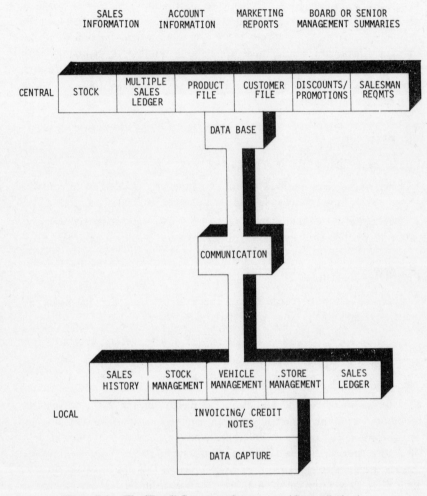

Figure 7.1   The 'Total' Customer System—a 'Constellation'

It can be seen from this chart that the inter-relationship of all the various activities to support a sale naturally flow into a complete system. We must consider this system if the maximum effect on profitability and influence of customers is to be realised. This group of activities naturally forms a 'constellation' which can be planned as a whole, although development and implementation can be phased into manageable sections. Following through the logic of Figure 7.1, the areas of their inter-dependence can be examined in more detail.

DATA CAPTURE

Data capture is the starting point without which no computerised system is possible. The means of data capture which is adopted depends on the way orders are taken and the organisation of the company. It is, however, absolutely vital, as, unless satisfactory data capture is achieved, there will be errors throughout the whole system and consequent customer irritation through either delivery inaccuracies or late delivery. It is not the purpose of this book to go into the technical means of data capture, except to state the general principle that as much as possible of this data involved in order taking, such as customer, order details, terms, should be 'validated' at or as near as possible to the original capture so that errors can be corrected promptly. The quicker this is done, the more effective the system.

For instance, at any time the system must be able to answer:

1. Is the customer number correctly identified?

2. Is it on file?

3. Are the products in stock? (This is a major area of customer irritation and ideally should be known at the original sales interview)

The GIGO principle 'garbage in, garbage out' is very relevant in the area of data capture for invoicing. In many instances a good total system has been wrecked due to failure to appreciate the data capture and validation requirements.

Apart from the vital necessity of accurate data capture, it is important to note that often up to 50% of the total system costs are associated with data capture and hence the method used needs careful evaluation in the light of its total cost. As far as possible, the least costly and most efficient systems are based on the order taker entering data into the machine. This can be at two levels:

1. The order taker is in direct contact with the computer and therefore full validation checks can be carried out at the time of ordering (such as customer number, products and their availability)

2. The order taker enters the data in a machine readable form that is not connected to the computer and hence validation checks are not possible.

INVOICING

Following naturally from data capture is the production of the warehouse order and invoice. Depending on the company, these can be the same or separate documents. The basic principles of invoicing are well understood but to achieve customer satisfaction and subsequent prompt payment, all relevant information must be included on the invoice with a satisfactory 'proof of delivery' system implemented so that subsequent customer queries can be actioned promptly and efficiently. A clear definition of products and packs should be made, and if the invoice is also used as a picking document the descriptions must be clear to the warehouse to ensure that the products and pack sizes requested are indeed selected and despatched along with correct costing. The computer gives the opportunity to have different product and pack sequences for selling and warehouse functions, which at times can be more efficient. For example an order-taking sequence may be requested for the customer but a picking document sequence will give more efficient handling in the warehouse.

Proof of delivery is an important area but a difficult one because the individual documents have to be stored either in their original form or on microfilm, as the signature of the customer is generally the only satisfactory proof of delivery. Storage of these original documents has to be in a form that allows easy retrieval when there is a proof of delivery query. It is sometimes possible to obtain delivery receipt numbers from larger customers, which can be entered into the computer system and quoted on any subsequent statements. At present there are no completely satisfactory means of taking copies of signatures and storing them in a computer with invoice data, and hence the storage of the original document or a microfilm equivalent is the only practical way of meeting the requirements of proof of delivery. An adequate total system in this area is of considerable importance as the loss in revenue associated with lack of proof can be substantial in a number of industries.

As can be seen from Figure 7.1, the total system is based on data capture and invoicing. Hence having achieved these functions the first level of information required at the basic selling and delivery unit (this may be national, regional or local) is the requirement to create the 'tools' to influence the customer. The same principles apply whether the selling is based on national, regional or local centres and only differ in scale and numbers. Computer systems which match the organisation of the company are now possible. This avoids large computer centralisation in companies which operate on a decentralised selling and delivery system. These tools can be summarised under the following headings:

Sales History

The requirement of sales history is one of the most hotly debated areas in industry. Just what information is required to influence the customer to purchase a larger quantity on the next delivery? Clearly the requirements of history depend on the type of product sold or service offered. In the area of one-off production previous history has little relevance, but where there are repeat orders for similar goods, particularly in consumer durables and consumables, previous history in some form is useful. Computer systems can give considerable help in this area, because all the information about previous orders is too voluminous to focus on the next selling occasion. Generally, the most appropriate information is summarised buying patterns and current trends. In addition to this, basic customer information is required and knowledge of the past use of special promotions and the way that the customer has reacted to them. Specific information on whether new products have penetrated the account also focuses the next sales interview. Such systems as these have to be tailored to the individual needs of the selling company, but can be very significant if a small amount of relevant information can focus the next sales interview in the areas where additional or more profitable sales can be achieved.

Other factors which are required to assist the selling interview are:

a. History of payment, so that cash can be collected where necessary or supply can be refused if the customer is registered as a bad payer

b. Information on special terms, such as quantity allowance, or co-operation allowance, so that this becomes a positive tool to help sell to the customer and to let him take maximum advantage of the company's terms. This results in the supplier obtaining the largest and most profitable order on minimum appropriate service arrangement

c. Knowledge of current availability of products being ordered, so that, where appropriate, substitutes can be provided for products temporarily out of stock or discontinued

To facilitate the building of a sales history the use of discrete geographical units, such as sales by grid squares or telephone sales areas, can be very useful if all other geographical definitions such as salesman area or delivery area are made up of a number of these units. By this means, as salesman areas or delivery areas change, the computer can still compare year by year performance for the newly defined geographical territory.

This then allows the sales organisation to regroup to attack the market with the computer still able to report relevant information.

Stock Management System

The stock management system flows naturally from data capture and invoicing, as nearly all the basic data to control stock is obtained from this function. By linking together local stock and sales this information can be transmitted to the central planning control of the company for the replenishment of stock. The advantage of a computer network is that stocks which may be held in various warehouses, at the factory or intermediately or in a local depot can all be brought together and full control be obtained by a planning group. The objectives of a stock management system are:

1. To improve cash flow and minimise interest on capital employed in financing stock

2. To keep the minimum stock and reduce the space required in warehouses and hence capital or rental costs for this space

3. To save clerical labour through the use of a computer system

A computerised system helps in this area in having complete and up-to-date information on all stock levels and sales, and ensures that the next replenishment has appropriate items. This reduces the safety stock required by reducing the time between stock leaving the warehouse and the replenishment arriving. It also forms the basis of forecasting future sales.

Store Management

Flowing naturally from data capture and the invoicing system is the picking document which governs the method of selection and overall warehouse control. There are different methods of warehouse management, which depend on type of business and lead time of orders. Principally, these can be divided into two areas, namely bulk vehicle loading and selection at the customer's premises or pre-selection in the warehouse to customer's order. The method used usually depends on the number of items which are delivered from each vehicle load. Generally the more the items the greater the efficiency of pre-selection of customer order in warehouse. In both instances, computerised systems assist in being able to produce bulk load summaries or individual picking documents in the most appropriate store sequence. Flowing from this, the picking document can be used by the computer to calculate standard times for warehouse selection and loading and summarise these as a management tool to minimise costs of handling.

Vehicle Management

With the steeply rising costs of drivers, vehicles and fuel it becomes an important item to control this activity to give the greatest productivity. The areas for optimisation are:

1. To give a full day's work within driving regulations (this becomes increasingly important with EEC regulations)

2. To give the most efficient route for the vehicle to minimise miles run

3. To ensure that the vehicle is not overloaded either for the driver's physical capacity or according to vehicle legislation

To achieve these objectives, it is necessary to be able to calculate standards for both delivery and driving, based on the invoice. There are a number of computer systems available on the market which can calculate optimum vehicle routes based on delivery time and average driving speeds. They can also take in a certain number of restrictions such as timed deliveries. Full systems are based on map references for the customer and knowledge of road distances in the geographical area concerned.

There are basically two types of problem which can be met by this system:

1. If sales for any day are completely random, the program has to optimise the deliveries and route as well as possible, based purely on geographical considerations and customer requirements. Special delivery requirements, lunchtimes and early closing can generally be included as factors around which a schedule is produced

2. A pattern of delivery can be established whereby certain areas are selected for delivery on only a few days each week. This generally results in greater optimisation of delivery service and careful consideration has to be given to customers who are serviced frequently to avoid additional journeys into any particular geographical area

In the first instance, the computer is working on all data each day. In the second, the computer can also help to establish an optimum pattern of delivery over a week or a fortnight in addition to the actual routing of the vehicle on each individual day. These complete computer systems are generally quite expensive in computer time and it has been found by a number of companies that most of the gains can be achieved by semi-computerised systems, which assign customers to areas and use the computer system to summarise delivery and driving time within each of those areas using a manual system to add areas together to a complete vehicle route.

The advantage of these computerised systems clearly depends on the previous efficiency of the manual system. Results in practice have often shown savings of up to 20% of mileage and 10% of vehicles.

Sales Ledger

All information required by the sales ledger flows naturally from the basic invoicing system, with information on customers and their orders. The problems associated with sales ledger are greatly improved by accurate invoicing and delivery. One of the major reasons for delays in payment are customers' queries. There are a few fundamental principles in the sales ledger which are worth listing:

1. Invoicing must be accurate

2. Delivery must be complete and accurate

3. Adequate proof of delivery must be obtained

4. Credit notes, where applicable, must clearly show the invoice to which they apply and must be issued promptly

5. Customers' queries must be answered by giving all the relevant information on invoices and statements e.g. customer's order number

The typical queries that delay payment are:

Proof of delivery required

Copy invoice required

Credit note required

Query on pricing

Query on discount

Query on special offers

Incorrect allocation of previous payments

The basic sales ledger and its requirements can be automatically updated from the invoicing system and the sales ledger organisation, based locally or centrally, depending on the method of trading, by the company concerned. Where there is a large number of multiple accounts requiring invoices at central paying offices, centralised systems often prove to be of advantage.

The payments received have to be posted and then allocated to individual accounts and invoices. A large proportion of payments is generally received with adequate identification as to the customer and the invoices being paid. There will, however, be a group of payments (in the writer's experience 15%–30%) where certain items relating to the payment will not be clear and therefore require special facilities to ensure quick turnround. Typical problems arise from:

Inadequate identification of customer (missing remittance details)

Invoices listed with wrong numbers or wrong dates

Payment which does not match any invoice

Part payments

Occasionally clerical time is wasted through:

Invoices paid twice

Payments to the wrong company

Overpayments

Computer systems to deal with the clearly defined payments work easily and effectively, but in the latter area special facilities are required to be able to examine customer and invoice details to enable matching and allocation of as much of the payment as possible. This is often carried out by means of visual display units which can display the total customer situation and enable effective 'conversation' between the accounts clerk and the computer. If visual display is not available then the original invoices will be required before work on unidentified payments can begin.

When the basic system is processed by the computer there is an added benefit from being able to obtain appropriate management information for sales ledger control and credit control. Examples of this are given in Figures 7.2 to 7.5.

Age (in weeks)/Number of accounts

Value (£'000)	1	2	3	4	5	6	7	8	9	10	11	12+
< 1	20	5	1	–	2	–	–	–	–	3	1	–
1– 2	10	10	4	3	1	2	3	1	–	–	–	–
2– 5	5	3	1	–	2	–	1	–	–	–	–	1
5–10	6	–	5	–	4	1	–	–	⑥	–	–	–
10–50	3	1	–	2	–	–	1	–	–	1	–	–
> 50	4	1	1	–	–	–	–	–	–	1	–	–

Figure 7.2 Debt Age Analysis—Multiple Accounts

Account		Total overdue
A3714C	Smith & Co.	£7,324·32
W7605P	Multistores	£25,196·09
R0619S	Jones Bros. Ltd.	£13,003·98
A1562B	*XYZ* Group	£6,110·03
D1916R	Freezefoods	£123,687·25
M6006W	Evanshops	£10,321·66

Figure 7.3 Debt Age Analysis—List of Accounts Owing £5,000 to £10,000 For Nine Weeks

District: Birmingham   *Parameter list*

Credit limit	£450
O/standing wks	5
Statement only	Yes
Type	Local
	Multiple

	Cr. limit	Oldest inv.		Last paid		Total O/S
W3711F						
J Smith & Sons	£500	3/5/75	£87·43	10/5/75	£162·40	£361·80
10 High St						
Walsall						
F3066P						
Quicksell	£700	20/4/75	£10·36	3/7/75	£303·20	£129·30
The Parade						
Leek						

Figure 7.4   Account Selections

			National average 3·4 wks	
District	*Sales this month*	*Ledger balance*	*Av. credit length (wks)*	*Av. credit length (wks) last month*
Liverpool	£512,163	£460,947	3·6	3·5
Birmingham	£603,269	£482,615	3·2	3·2
Glasgow	£631,146	£599,494	3·8	3·8
Bristol	£486,344	£413,392	3·4	3·5

Figure 7.5   Administration Centre Performance—Average Credit Lengths

Figure 7.2 demonstrates a typical overall debt age analysis, showing the number of accounts by value outstanding in a matrix of size of order and age in weeks. Resulting from 7.2 a typical request is shown in Figure 7.3 relating to the six accounts having a value of £5,000–£10,000 which are nine weeks old. The actual customer and total amount overdue is shown in Figure 7.3 for investigation and follow-up. Figure 7.4 displays a selection of accounts, showing credit limit, their oldest invoice, the last invoice that has been paid and the overall outstanding balance. This is a useful facility, when readily available, giving information to the representative or credit controller on his next visit to the customer. Figure 7.5 is a typical overall control where there is decentralised responsibility for the collection of cash, giving overall results in average credit lengths in numbers of weeks, comparing districts and their performance with previous months and national average.

As can be readily seen, this type of information makes appropriate management activity possible in the sales ledger and enables quick identification of any customer who has been overlooked in the basic routines of the system.

A well-designed system with adequate follow-up has been proved to reduce credit, which at current interest rates and the overall business problem of cash flow, is important to every business. It will be found in general that the justification for a computerised sales ledger system will be a combination of clerical savings and reduced interest on working capital.

DATA BASE

Each company requires a base of data relating to customers, products, discounts, selling performance and account performance, so that analyses can be produced which focus sales and marketing management on opportunity areas. Dealing first with the data, the following areas should be considered.

Customers

Basic information on customers, their names and addresses and relevant sales information as to the type of outlet and its main purpose of business should be collected by sales representatives and fed into the system in a positive and realistic way. The major problem with the customer file is that it tends to get out of date, with the field force not actioning changes on the central files. This system needs to be very carefully considered, as the whole basis of information will be put in jeopardy by shoddy maintenance of the customer file. It should be one of the objectives of sales management to check the details of accounts with representatives and ensure that they are accurate.

Product File

The product file contains all details of products, such as price, methods of packing and special prices for quantities etc. Generally, it is better to have a number of scales so that each customer can be individually flagged for his appropriate scale. If, however, there is a very large number of scales the only practical method may be to make it part of the customer record. Price files have to include dates of price revisions, as subsequent reports and credit notes have to be based on the price which applied in a previous time period.

Current developments in America and the Continent of a universal product code (UPC) will help gain the full advantages of computerised systems where there is a common language of customer number and product number between supplier and customer. This also opens the possibility of computer readable documentation passing to the customer to avoid paperwork and data capture costs.

Associated with UPC is the use of symbols on all packages so that optical scanning is possible at 'check outs' giving immediate pricing or subsequent information for stock control and replenishment planning.

Discounts and Promotions

The full range of the company's discounts and promotions has to be entered into the customer file to ensure accurate application in each sale. The advantages of computerisation in this area are that the correct rates are applied and the full benefit of the marketing activity can be realised. It also gives the opportunity to calculate the true cost of any promotional activity associated with the sales gains.

Other Classifications

It is necessary to ensure that the customer file has sufficient classifications such as salesmen, depot of supply, geographical area, trade group, class of business, so that different analyses which focus on one particular feature can be carried out subsequently and enable special action to be taken to improve its performance.

INFORMATION OBTAINABLE FROM THE DATA BASE

There are a number of computer packages on the market to assist in the formulation of a data base. They need to be carefully evaluated in the light of the true needs of the company so that sufficient information will be available and yet the costs in computer time be justifiable on the basis of the improvement in selling and marketing of the company's products or services.

Once having established the data base, it is possible to obtain any significant information about the customers that is required to run the business. The data base enables any appropriate correlation of features and sales which have been designed into the system. This assumes that adequate data capture, both of invoice detail and of static information about the customer, has been completed satisfactorily.

The major information areas which can be obtained from the data base, assuming that the necessary accounting and planning data have already been extracted as described, are sales information, account management information, marketing information and summary information for board decisions, as appropriate.

SALES INFORMATION

The available information on sales can be presented in many ways. The following are typical:

1. Sales by time period against target, both weekly and cumulative showing the different divisions or regions of the sales force. It is often sensible to limit the more detailed information to the more important items or products and to summarise the rest

2. Product sales are often sensibly presented in product groups and their performance in different trade areas. This should be presented as actual and standard so that the strength of sales in certain trade sectors is not being balanced by poor performance in others

3. Analysis of individual accounts and the penetration of the product range can direct selling activity to existing customers who are not taking advantage of all the company's product range or services offered

4. Inactive accounts. A list of inactive customers who previously traded with the company is a trigger for action to investigate the reasons for the loss of trade

5. An area which repays some experimentation is that of comparing sales methods to judge effectiveness compared with cost. It has been previously mentioned that there are a number of different methods of selling which apply to most companies and few have investigated the true effects of changing sales methods. Controlled experiments can be set up, with both the current system and the trial systems over a given period, which match effectiveness of the different methods of selling. An example of this is shown in Figure 7.6, which is comparing telephone selling with personal calls in two areas within a seasonal business. The advantage of comparison is that outside influences such as seasonality or competitor activity, provided it is similar in both areas, are equivalent and hence the increase or decrease in sales is directly measurable between the control and test group. In the example shown, sales were increased by 19% by changing the sales method. By subsequent accountant activity, the costs of the two methods can be compared with the additional margin on sales. This demonstrates the advantage of a good data base and its use for more special exercises when reorganising the national sales effort of an individual company

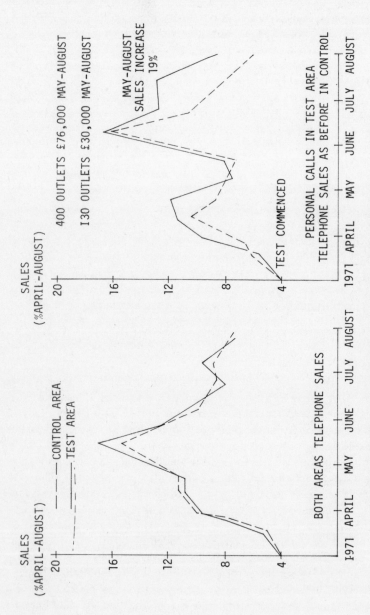

Figure 7.6 Comparison of Selling with Personal Calls and Telephone Sales

6. At the individual salesman's daily sales level, local reports are useful depending on the nature of sales, which compare daily performance in two areas: (i) overall sales, and (ii) specific sales of promoted or selected items. Regular analysis on a daily basis, at local level, of each salesman or saleswoman, showing the number of productive calls and total sales, together with their targets for those particular customers, keeps constant attention on the real objective and indicates quickly to local sales management the areas of difficulty. In the second area, the computor helps in producing specific analyses of specially promoted lines, showing quantities sold and penetration into individual accounts by sales agents, hence showing where there are any particular problems on a short time scale.

ACCOUNT INFORMATION

Typical reports available from the data base are:

1. The services or products purchased by each customer, comparing time periods, analysing by value growth and achievement against target

2. Account summaries of larger customers with more than one outlet or place of business, showing the performance of each individual outlet for subsequent discussion with national or regional management, with a view to bringing up the poorer to the best standards

3. Analysis of delivery size and type, by customer, so that opportunities for saving on the cost of distribution can be fully realised

4. Performance by account, in relation to representative or sales management, to show performance by individual selling agent over time periods compared with previous performance and target

5. Sales of services or products, by customer, showing opportunities for increased sales

6. Discount reports by account, so that true knowledge of total discount from standard price given away to each customer is known and acted upon. This has to be analysed by all the various types of discount which a company may be offering

7. Credit summaries have already been mentioned. They can be added to this list of information available from the full data base

8. Special promotion reports, where the results of promotions are analysed by customer and cost

9. Account profitability. This is little understood in most businesses because there is a tremendous variation in the profitability of customers when the full range of factors affecting it are analysed. A typical spread of profitability is shown in Figure 7.7

Figure 7.7 demonstrates the possibility of improvement. If all accounts can be brought up to the half-way line, considerable extra profit will be generated within the organisation. As this figure shows, there is a range from nil profitability to 35%, measured as contribution as a percentage of turnover. This is not an unusual pattern for many companies trading with a range of customers.

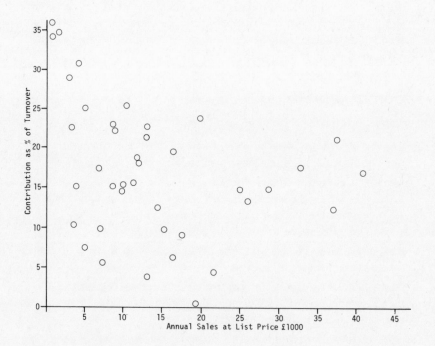

Figure 7.7   Example of variation in Consumer Profitability as Percentage of Sales (Sample of Commercial, Wholesale, Institutional and Industrial Customers)

The computer can help in that with a large number of customers and the many different factors that make up the cost of sales, a regular monitoring of profitability is very difficult by any manual means. Figure 7.8 gives an example of a typical computer output for account profitability, giving the different areas where special costs are incurred. From customer to customer there is a very different contribution to profit. Regular monitoring of this, together with action by management, is another way in which the computer helps to increase profitability.

	Fourth quarter		Year to date	
	£	%	£	%
Sales at list price	100	33·3	350	50·0
Others at list price	200	66·7	350	50·0
Total at list price	300	100·0	700	100·0
General terms cost	24	8·0	75	10·7
Other terms cost	28	9·3	50	7·1
Total terms cost	52	17·3	125	17·8
Gross sales value	248	82·7	575	82·2
Ex works cost	186	62·0	435	62·2
Gross profit	62	20·7	140	20·0
Less sales costs:				
Overrider	5	1·7	13	1·9
Bonus	4	1·3	10	1·4
Promotions	2	0·7	4	0·6
Sales Force	3	1·0	8	1·1
Telesales	1	0·3	3	0·4
Special sales agent cost	--	0·0	–	0·0
Distribution	10	3·3	25	3·6
Excess credit	2	0·7	2	0·3
Total variable cost	27	9·0	65	9·3
Cash contribution	35	11·7	75	10·7
Distribution overheads	6	2·0	15	2·1
Sales admin.	2	0·7	5	0·7
Terms credit	4	1·3	9	1·3
Total overhead cost	12	4·0	29	4·1
Total sales cost	39	13·0	94	13·4
CONTRIBUTION TO PROFIT	23	7·7	46	6·6

Figure 7.8 Profit Statement For Specific Customer

MARKETING REPORTS

Marketing reports are specifically concerned with products and services and their performance. Typical reports are:

1. Regular reports on products and their performance actual and planned, so that decisions can be made on dropping poor lines, introducing new products, promotions and any other special activities required
2. Reports on particular performance in different trade sectors. These identify any changes in product or pack or service that may be required to improve any particular trade area

3. Cumulative product profit analyses which show actuals and variance by product with the changes in costs of original purchase or manufacture, along with added value costs so that a constant and realistic pricing basis can be maintained

4. Accounts purchasing habits by products are required both by individual outlets and by trade groups to direct advertising or changes in products when necessary.

BOARD OR SENIOR MANAGEMENT SUMMARIES

The advantage of a computer system is that the individual reports required at each level can be summarised to give the overall trends of the business, such as:

1. Product or service summaries, showing performance by marketing group in a time period with actuals and variances from plan. This may show quantities or turnover as appropriate to the individual business

2. Trading summaries, which give a performance by sector, with actuals and variances from plan, indicating direct trading profit and profit per unit of sale

3. Distribution control. The comparison of tonnage delivered by trade sector with planned source of deliveries. This is particularly useful in decisions between direct, depot or wholesale delivery

4. Other summaries which are derived from the total summarisation of those mentioned under selling, accounts and marketing above

As can be seen from this brief outline a total structure of information is possible, which reduces to a minimum duplication and cost and yet focuses management selling and marketing activity on where to influence the customer.

Most companies, in practice, have developed their total customer information system in a piecemeal manner, which has not used the interlinks and dependencies of information to achieve a total system which is both consistent and at the right level of detail for the management's tasks. While total information systems and data bases are probably too sophisticated for most companies, an approach which recognises 'constellations' of related activity and designs a total computer system around them will obtain the maximum advantages from computerisation. It is important not to be over-ambitious and yet to design the system's logical links even if all parts of it represent a number of years computer development programme. In this area, a forward plan of computer developments over a three- or five-year period, with the total design understood, will save considerably in development activity and in the end reduce overall operating costs of the system and ensure the most appropriate and accurate information. The computer system, however well designed and operated, is only a 'tool' which must be used by management and sales staff in a sensible manner to achieve results. In every area it is vital that a full training programme is part of the computer system and that management accept it as part of their management style. The understanding of the use of information and a style of management that accepts it is often quite difficult to overcome within the established methods of operation within a concern.

The system itself will only be tuned by the constant use of its results for specific action, and, where they are found to be inaccurate, a follow-up on the reason why, such as faulty data capture, or erroneous customer information entered into the system by the selling agent.

With the introduction of this constellation approach, a senior manager must be made responsible for the entire information system as it has ramifications within a number of line functions, such as sales, marketing, accounts, planning, procurement etc. Within a normal business this co-ordination would only be possible by the chairman or chief executive himself. It is, therefore, important to establish a senior information manager, who co-ordinates the total activity, ensures that all parties work to the rules and also get the maximum gain from the information which emerges from the system. The information itself should be presented in a form which demands action not just interest, and is the regular basis of performance discussions between management and those responsible for each individual function.

CHAPTER 8

Production and Materials Control

BY M. THORNLEY AND D. GRAHAM

MANAGEMENT USE OF COMPUTERS FOR PRODUCTION CONTROL

The managers of any manufacturing business need a production control function to obtain and use information on the demand for the product or service, planned and achieved use of the work force and plant, inventory planning and control, and the scheduling of work loads. In times of scarce and limited investment it is especially important to achieve the most profitable use of all corporate resources and in manufacturing, the production control function fulfils this key role.

Accurate and timely information being the essential feature of production control, it follows that the use of computers (information processing machines) has been proposed almost since the introduction of computers into business enterprises. It is disappointing to see that, notwithstanding the significant capital investment in computers in manufacturing businesses, the results in many companies are insubstantial. The problems are well known, nevertheless few companies have realised major benefits. Sophisticated control systems alone do not provide the answer; what is essential is accurate problem diagnosis and expert management of both the business and the computer. In large companies a high level of business expertise is more often available and such companies provide most of the examples of successful application of computers in production control. However, it should not be inferred that some small and medium-size companies are not also successful, indeed such companies frequently have entrepreneurial and management talent of a high order, but it has to be recognised that implementing a computer system in production control will have a profound effect on the company and require a significant amount of skilled management time during the development and implementation periods. This must be provided and if, as may be the case in the smaller companies, resources of the requisite quality and skill are not available, then the alternatives are either to recruit staff with required skill and experience, or to hire consultant staff who work *for* and *with* the permanent management.

Failure to involve the necessary quantity and quality of management is the most frequent cause of the disappointments encountered when 'computerisation' of production control is attempted.

There is a powerful case for the use of computers in most manufacturing businesses. However, it is essential that the environment, and the problems and advantages of 'computerisation' be carefully studied to arrive at a logically reasoned decision and the correct course of action. This chapter reviews the main considerations and illustrates them by examples of success and failure in the expectation that the readers will emulate the successes and learn to avoid the failures.

BUSINESS CHARACTERISTICS

Manufacturing businesses can be classified into types according to the nature of their manufacturing activity. This is convenient as within each group problems and solutions are similar and relate to the same basic concepts. For the purposes of present consideration the following classifications are proposed:

Process industry	e.g. Petro-chemicals, pharmaceuticals and foods
Flow line production	e.g. Automobile assembly, electronics
Batch production	e.g. Light engineering, electronic assembling and optics
Jobbing	e.g. Heavy capital equipment, shipbuilding and 'one-offs'
Service and repair	e.g. Automobile, electrical
Factoring	e.g. Wholesaling, consumer durables, food

In some businesses there may be a mixture of these processes, formalised by a divisional structure e.g. 'manufacturing', and 'warehouse and distribution'. It is important to consider the functions objectively as a good compromise will only be reached when the requirements and limitations of each function are taken into account in the system design and implementation.

It must also be recognised that different businesses have a functional bias which requires a corresponding emphasis in a computer system serving the enterprise. An example is a factoring business, where the company is dominated by sales and marketing staff who have objectives of customer service, achieved by good inventory performance and sales order processing. However, in a company producing high technology optical products the dominant group is R & D, which is designing and producing small quantities of expensive, technically sophisticated products.

APPLICATION AREAS

It is a sad reflection of managerial ability, in the short history of the use of computers in business, that most of the computer systems were developed for each business function in isolation. In such cases the priorities were decided by the dominant functional group in the business, or by the function receiving (but not necessarily deserving) most of the blame for the company's ills, or finally and worst of all, the 'decibel' system: he who shouts loudest and most often gets attention to reduce the noise.

The illogicality of this approach has long been recognised by the major computer manufacturers who, having a vested interest in the successful application of computers, produced business systems concepts and 'application packages' which considered the totality of the business function. Initially these concepts had little credibility, in part because some computer salesmen, with only a superficial knowledge of business problems, oversold the equipment and system capability. In part also, many managements reading the glossy sales manuals abdicated their managerial responsibility to so-called computer experts. The lesson has been painfully learned. The computer manufacturers now publish their concepts proposals in more humble and practical terms which help user managements to produce an application framework and a strategy for their investment in computing. A good example of such a conceptual approach is published by IBM under the title 'COPICS' (Communications Orientated Production Information and Control System, G320–1230).

RATIONALE

As business has developed from the cottage industry when one man controlled the day-to-day business, enterprises have become more expensive and difficult to manage. Capital investment and inventory investment increase with size and the problem of co-ordinating resources and minimising the divergence between a manager's personal and corporate objectives is increasingly complex. A company is successful when it can collate, interpret and issue the information necessary to the operation of the business. As any 'owner-manager' knows, the road to ruin is littered with the wrecks of those who ran a complex activity by information which was increasingly incomplete and out of date if not downright irrelevant. It is essential to recognise the point at which the lack of essential control and administrative information is becoming a handicap leading to a danger, and take action. This action, at a point in the growth of the company, will include the use of a computer to process manufacturing and inventory information.

RESPONSIBILITY

When the corporate management decide on computer processing for their information it is vital for them to realise (and to act on the concept) that this is the starting point of a new management responsibility and not an abdication of responsibility. The responsibility cannot be left to 'computer experts' who have a 'systems bias'. Their technical knowledge must be guided by sound business judgement and knowledge. It follows that in allocating line managers to such a project the frequent scheme of putting forward 'old Fred who is a good committee man and knows all our products' is a recipe for disaster. Management involvement means the active participation of the chief executive and a selection of the management high-fliers who will recognise that their contribution to the success of the computer project furthers their own and the company's successful development.

PRODUCTION CONTROL FUNCTIONS

An analysis of the nature of the business will produce a number of headlines which are production control functions. It is necessary to identify which of these are required, the relative significance of each to the business and the advantages and disadvatages of using a computer system to process each function's information. The following are examples of production control activities: (i) sales, marketing and production liaison; (ii) production program planning and development; (iii) inventory recording; (iv) capacity and labour planning; (v) material planning and provisioning; (vi) expediting; (vii) factory scheduling, releasing and work progress; and (viii) physical storage and security. It will be noted that the word 'control' does not appear in the list. Two principles for not using a computer to 'control' production are:

1. Decison rules executed by a computer system are essentially of yes/no options. This produces an inflexible system which is not readily modified to meet new situations. Such is acceptable in the mathematical world but nowhere else

2. It is a manager's job to reach decisions based on objective and subjective criteria. The purpose of a computer system is to provide the data for some of the objective criteria. This principle should not be taken too literally—it does not mean only the production director can decide to buy a replacement stock of split pins—nor does it mean that the figures on machine load produced by the computer are proof incontrovertible that the company must review its production facilities.

INVENTORY

Inventory is one of the first areas to which computers were applied in business, and this sector is the scene of some spectacular successes and some sad failures. Inventory as defined by the British Production and Inventory Control Society is:

> Stock-keeping items which are held in a stock point and which serve to decouple successive operations in the process of manufacturing a product and distributing it to the consumer. Inventories may consist of finished goods ready for sale, they may be parts or intermediate products, or they may be raw materials. The basic decoupling function of inventories has two aspects:

> 1. Inventories necessary because it takes time to complete an operation and to move the product from one stage to another i.e. in-process and movement inventories
> 2. Inventories employed for organisational reasons such as to let one unit schedule its operations more or less independently of another i.e. organisational inventories

Inventories are a company's decoupling response to demand and it is important to recognise that demands differ in nature. In some industries the demand is linked closely to production planning, in others, e.g. factoring and wholesaling, demand is directly related to customer demand only.

FACTORING AND WHOLESALING INVENTORIES: INDEPENDENT DEMAND

The primary functions, which are suited to computer application, are inventory recording and reporting i.e. how much of which items are stocked where, and when they should be re-ordered. The forecasting techniques which are suitable have been described in an earlier chapter. Two principal approaches to reviewing inventory in this statistical manner are used:

1. Fixed time review i.e. once per period (week/month) the inventory master file is examined by the system and a calculation is made to determine how many of each item should be re-ordered to restore inventory availability to a pre-set desired operating level
2. Fixed quantity review i.e. on each transaction run the available balance is compared with a safety level and a pre-set re-order quantity is requested if necessary to restore the inventory to the desired level

The first method produces a regular flow of orders for variable quantities and requires judgement to balance the speed of response, frequency of stock-outs, against the cost of orders and handling small quantities.

The second method responds more quickly but depends on the supplier's ability to match an erratic demand pattern and puts a variable load on purchasing, accounting and warehousing.

Computers were applied to this situation early in their introduction to business. This method of inventory 'control', using various statistical techniques, is very successful in the right environment; unfortunately computer salesmen sold this methodology into manufacturing: a different environment. This was the source of many of the failures which wrongly discredited both the technique and the application of EDP. The failures resulted from the failure of management, particularly production control managers, to assume the leadership and responsibility for designing a system fitted to the needs of the business. The trap into which they fell was that they assigned more importance to the method than to the goal and thus the means dominated the ends. It is necessary to recognise that 'dependent demand' situations require a totally different solution to the factoring/retailing solutions, consequently to use statistical material control methodology will at best be most unsatisfactory and ineffective. Experience has shown it to result in near or actual disasters.

There is, it follows, a different requirement in manufacturing inventory control which must be set in the context of the manufacturing activity.

MANUFACTURING APPLICATIONS—DEPENDENT DEMAND

The most comprehensive use of computing in manufacturing occurs in batch manufacturing which will now be used as a basis of development for our theme. The use of a computer can only be meaningfully discussed in the context of its application—in this case a production control system. A computer system can be effective only when the underlying concepts are sound, it will not create good management or a better business. It is essential that a valid control system is first provided, not by systems analysts, but by involving senior line management. Systems analysts cannot be expected to learn new professions: accounting, marketing, or production control. It is the sphere of the professional manager to focus the business system.

Early attempts to produce production and inventory control (P & IC) systems were based on 'surveys' where the existing system was studied and then emulated because the survey team was conditioned to the old system of thinking. This was rarely a successful approach.

The second development alternative was the 'blank cheque—ask them what they want' approach. This was even less successful and more time consuming. Junior levels of line management are not skilled in communicating or conceptual thinking; in fact, frequently they do not know what they want or need. The results were usually diverging flights of fancy and eventual disenchantment of most individuals with the end product.

The approach now favoured is to design a system for tomorrow (not two or five years hence) and for tomorrow's business based on the needs of the business. This requires a study of the market, manufacturing environment and a brief survey of the management's responsibilities and administrative procedures to understand the working of the company. Senior management who understand and have the vision to develop this picture are vital to the production of this basic outline. An excellent prescription for systems planning for production and inventory control is given in a paper by J. A. Orlicky presented at APICS national conference, Philadelphia, 1966 and published in Europe by BPICS. Dr. Orlicky supports the 'black box' method in which line managers assume that 'the box' will do everything they tell it to do. They postulate the input and outputs. The systems analysts and programmers take the lid off the 'black box' and determine what must be put inside to make it work. There are series of 'black boxes' dealing with the various levels of input and outputs. This will identify impracticalities where the implementation would be impossible because the input and outputs are postulated too ambitiously or too ambiguously. Thus the technologists refine the detail of the system without losing the overall objective.

PRODUCTION CONTROL MANAGEMENT

The production control manager requires a series of functions:

Customer order service.   As with the factor he needs to relate the demand for his product or stock to his ability to supply that demand effectively, which leads to:

Master scheduling planning.   This is a statement of future requirements identified by product, date and quantity which in turn needs:

Material requirements planning.   To answer the questions: what do we need to produce? from what bought-in supplies? how much and when do we need them? This requires three further functions:

Engineering data: How do we manufacture this item? What components and materials make this item?

Resource requirements planning: Which plant, equipment and assembly facilities are required? What is the load and required date on each facility?

Inventory planning: What levels of inventory (of which kind) give a good compromise between customer service and manufacturing resource efficiency?

Kitting, releasing and shortage reporting. What batches of work should be released to the shop and are the requisite items available? if not what are the shortages and why?

Shop floor control. Recording the movement of work through the manufacturing facility and the variations of manufacturing capacity availability.

Purchasing and receiving. The initiation, monitoring, progress and receipt of purchased requirements which may be physical goods or sub-contracted services.

SYSTEMS IMPLEMENTATION PLANNING

The list of functions mentioned above form, in a company of only modest size, a substantial programme of work. It is necessary to formulate within the total strategy an implementation plan which considers (i) the relative priorities of the various parts of the system, (ii) the short and intermediate-term payback of each part, (iii) the resources available for implementation, (iv) the logical inter-relationships and inter-dependencies of the parts, and (v) the quality of the data currently available. An MIS (management information system) should be viewed as the cream obtained when the financial, administrative, operations control and engineering systems are operational. That is, first build basic foundations and progress forward only when assured that each modular function is consolidated as an effective and secure operation.

APPLICATION DESCRIPTIONS

It is usual to select either inventory recording/accounting or engineering data control as the logical start point of a P & IC system; however, a well-conceived plan will anticipate the need for a data base common to all the sub-systems. Most of the computer manufacturers, management consultants and software houses can provide a 'data base' computer package. The sales promotions suggest a greater disparity in quality of these packages than in reality exists between the principal contenders. This is probably influenced by the limitations of resources, in-house staff experience and the desire to recoup or build on past investment. The rule of 'caveat emptor' applies. The buyer of an 'off the peg' suit must use his business sense and judgement to take a view of the practicability, extent and cost of tailoring the general package and whether the end result gives an acceptable solution to his needs. The best advice is to find several users (not only those selected by the salesmen), meet the user staff on their ground and listen to their past and present problems and then check the level of support given by the supplier. An example of these applications installed by the writer provides a framework to identify specific problems showing how in one instance a suitable solution was implemented.

The application concerned contracts for manufacturing electronic systems for military use and the problem of materials provisioning was assuming large proportions. A computer system was proposed and accepted. The advice was to start with a Bill of Material Processor (BOMP) and develop the subsequent systems from the base. An existing 'packaged' data base system supplied by International Business Machines Ltd. was chosen because:

a. It provided for current requirements and future developments

b. There was available experience of using a similar package

c. A suitable computer for the package was available and thus no major additional computer hardware expenditure was required

d. The package was already proven in use, and experience of the supplier indicated that the capability, capacity and willingness to assist with its use were reliable and not prohibitively expensive

BILLS OF MATERIAL PROCESSING

The package provided a file manipulation and control facility for a number of associated files. The system in this case centred on five files:

1. The Item Master File (also termed Part Number Master File, PNMF)

2. Product Structure File (PSF)

3. Work Centre Master File

4. Product Routing File

5. Subordinate Part Number Master File

The Item Master is the key data base file to which the other files are related and by which in most cases the other files are accessed by the subordinate systems. The first application, that of 'exploding' a finished stock item into gross requirements of the required constituent items, will illustrate the functioning of the Item Master File (PNMF) and the Product Structure File (PSF).

The first part of the business to which the system was applied was concerned with manufacturing small quantities of large and complex items in a 'made to order' environment i.e. zero stockholding. When the order was received the drawing and design offices set to work to specify the product as illustrated in Figure 8.1. Frequently modules and assemblies which had been designed for previous products were used. Initially the drawing office parts lists were transcribed and made suitable for data

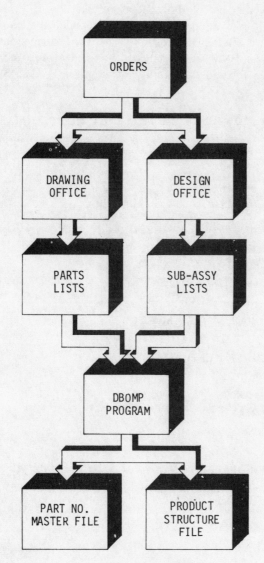

Figure 8.1

entry (subsequently, by creating special editor programs, the original document was used). The input data was used by the package to create and maintain the PNMF and PSF files.

An abbreviated list of the contents of the PNMF record is shown in Figure 8.2. Not all the 'fields' shown contained data at this stage nor were all required. This redundancy is often experienced when using a package. The PNMF file contained fields generated and used by the control system for addressing and validating the Product Structure File.

PRINCIPAL CONTENTS OF THE PART NUMBER MASTER FILE

FIELD NAME

PART NUMBER
DESCRIPTION
ISSUE NUMBER
ITEM TYPE
FIXED ORDER QUANTITY
MINIMUM ORDER QUANTITY
MAXIMUM ORDER QUANTITY
ORDER QUANTITY MULTIPLE
PRODUCTION LEAD TIME
PURCHASE LEAD TIME
ORDER POLICY
UNIT COST
MATERIAL COST
LABOUR COST
OVERHEAD COST
FIRST SUPPLIER AND CATALOGUE NUMBER
SECOND SUPPLIER AND CATALOGUE NUMBER
RE-ORDER POINT
LINE OF MANUFACTURE
SAFETY STOCK
UNIT OF MEASURE
ALTERNATIVE UNIT OF MEASURE
CONVERSION FACTOR
EFFECTIVITY DATE

Figure 8.2

Some of these fields were:

First assembly component address: to give the disc address of the first component in the structure of this item

Record count: the count of the number of structure levels in this assembly used for audit and control

First assembly 'where used' address: for the next higher level assembly

Low level code: the lowest level at which this item occurs in all product structures

First routing address: start of the 'how it is manufactured' methodology

Address of first sub-part number master file record

At this stage the system could explode a stock item through the various levels of assemblies and components to reach raw materials and bought-in items. There are generally, as in this instance, three 'types' of explosion:

Single-level explosion where the item is broken down into its constituent components and assemblies

Indented explosion which breaks each sub-assembly within assembly into its constituents, listing each new structure level number

Summarised explosion which is the most useful function as it summarises the total quantity of each component in a given product and is used also in the material standard costing systems

Also available were a similar series of three 'implosions' which indicated the 'where-used, goes-into or used-on' relationships in a similar fashion.

The original package was modified to include an 'item-type' field. One of the purposes of this was to identify an item as:

Finished goods

Assembly made in works

Components made in works

Purchased item

Raw material

The extension of this classification will be explained later. At this stage it was possible to produce a series of four requisitions resulting from one contract. These are shown in Figure 8.1. The two purchase requisitions initiated supply action in the form of purchase orders. Similarly, the 'made-in-works' items initiated production control action for the machine shop and assembly departments. The re-order point listing shown in Figure 8.3 was not available in the original package. Initially, we decided it would be uneconomic to use expensive computer time to carry out detailed planning for low value, low usage items (the 'C' stores of the well-known ABC classification of stores). We knew, however, that the statistical basis of re-order point control postulated relatively even usage with control limits, over time. In fact the situation is that this demand or usage is very 'lumpy' i.e. the usage may be coasting at say between 20 and 30 items per month most of the year but at an unpredictable point would jump to say 1,500 and subsequently return to the previous rate. It was out of the question to set re-order levels to cover the 'lumpy' demand since, notwithstanding the low unit value of the items, the range of items to be covered was extremely large, consequently the inventory investment would have been prohibitive.

We have adopted a simple bin card which recorded the re-order point, re-order quantity and stock balance. In brief terms, the storekeeper checks the computer requisition against his bin cards, and if the quantity requisitioned would reduce his stock below re-order point he creates an order using a 'manual requisition'. Two significant advantages this approach produced were:

1. A reduction of production delays due to stock-outs despite lower inventory levels
2. Considerable reduction of inventory obsolescence, originally due to excessive inventory levels

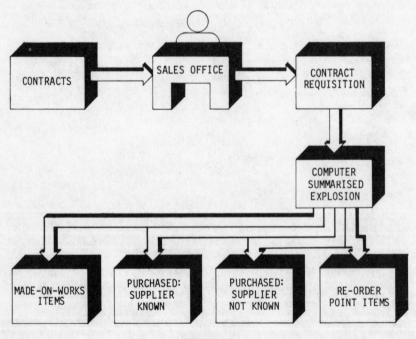

Figure 8.3

MASTER SCHEDULE PLANNING

In a business which primarily depends on its ability to produce a range of products to sell at competitive prices, using a common set of resources, one of the main resources is investment in inventory. Indeed one frequently notes in company balance sheets that inventory (often erroneously called stock) is the largest single asset. High-powered committees indulge in corporate politics deciding which unit can have expensive new items of plant, while a lowly clerk in production control issues instructions to spend the same amount of money every working week of his life. This situation occurs in many manufacturing companies and demonstrates mis-allocation of management time. It would be more sensible to put effort and resource into the expenditure incurred in purchasing the right items at the right time at a reasonable price thus affording the possibility of using the existing production facility most effectively. In most manufacturing in-volving fabrication and assembly this means first 'materials planning' and subsequently 'shop scheduling'. Materials planning logically has to start from the point of what do we need to make, how many and by when? That is the master schedule. Unfortunately, this expression is used in an ambig-uous way. The definition widely accepted (see BPICS dictionary) is 'A broad schedule of the total number of units to be produced in the future specifying the dates and quantity required'.

It is common to find a number of procedures for loading production requirements onto the master schedule even within a single manufacturing unit since demand can originate from:

Contracts

Specific customer orders

Stock authorisations (to meet sales and market forecasts)

Inter-plant orders

Special works orders e.g. items for works use

The master schedule system should embody information from warehouse stock balances, outstanding customer orders, projected and forecast demand. It is often the case that the master schedule planning module is dynamic, and changes daily. One might think of it as a movie film, each 'frame' being different as forecasts, demand call off, and stocks change. Rush orders for special customer requirements or spares for field maintenance can be inserted into the master schedule plan at short notice and even within the standard manufacturing lead time of the requested item. One important point to remember is that the farther into the future the forecast is extended the less certain and reliable it becomes.

The primary use of master schedule planning is to provide the input to the inventory management module. In the example being considered the printed format of the master schedule (called in this case 'PRODUC-TION PLAN') was used as the basis of regular progress meetings between production control management and sales management to review changes of requirements and highlight failures to meet agreed schedules.

The next major step in the management's plan in our example was to use a computer system to handle the 'book-keeping' chores of materials planning originating from the master schedule plan. Implementing this decision followed the stages now described.

INVENTORY RECORDING

Inventory planning and inventory recording are sub-systems being part of the hierarchy of the materials requirements planning (MRP) system. The most basic is inventory recording (sometimes called inventory accounting). Conceptually it is the most simple step—in fact it can produce almost traumatic shock as production control staff re-orientate their thinking and work methods from the traditional manual stock record card. The essentials consist of transferring and verifying (by stock counting) stock card record balances to computer records and thereafter maintaining the records accurately by processing all the transactions. A word of caution is appropriate since the writer's experience is that a 'manual system', in fact (at least in enterprises which have been operating a number of years) consists of two systems.

The formal system. Documented in production control and accounting departments. Manuals are often out of date, but usually define most of the transactions, the authorising staff, distribution and effect of the documentation.

The informal system. Which is the actual use made of documents in the system. This needs very careful investigation by skilled staff who know the subject. Frequent problems encountered are:

1. 'Fields' on the documents not completed or not required
2. Documents used for differing functions in different departments and the stock record clerk 'interpreting' appropriate function on each occasion
3. Two different documents with overlapping or identical functions and no clear differentiation
4. Documents used to record transactions other than those specified (a typical shop floor gambit to disguise excess issues)
5. Document distribution (including unofficial extra copies) which varies from those specified in the manual

The design and specification of an inventory recording computer system is consequently a task requiring a lot of skill and knowledge since the resulting inventory information is to be used for the complex computer processing involved. Not only production control, but also accounting, goods receiving, purchasing, warehousing, inspection, sales office and the shop floor have essential requirements and interests to be considered, protected and catered for. The specification should take account of these many needs and the problems of editing to filter out errors which would destroy the credibility of the results. Knowledge of the broader picture of production control and business systems is essential to ensure that the system will be capable of meeting the full requirement. Generally it is advisable to have a modular design where a number of sub-routines can be called if needed. This set of routines consists of both common and unique procedures and should be expandable by additional routines to meet new requirements without the need to re-write large sections of programs.

The control of input data and error recovery is a substantial manual task which not only requires design and extensive documentation but, most necessarily, a thorough understanding arising from comprehensive education of the staff who contribute to the system. Neglect of this education is a common cause of problems but systems cannot be isolated from the people who work with them. Thus not only must the systems be related to the level and quality of staff employed, they must be seen to contribute to the improvement of the work task.

Information relating to balances on hand (of inventory), total outstanding orders, inventory allocated are maintained in the item master file; however this 'balance forward' method will cause difficulties when the results do not correspond to the contributing transactions. This can be resolved by accumulating a file of transactions. In the example used in a Rank Organisation manufacturing unit, all the transactions are recorded during the 'process run' on the 'back-up file', from which, on request, the users can scan a sequential record in part number sequence of the transactions in date sequence. This provides a better audit trail than the usual printed proof list of each day's (or batch of) transactions which, because of the random sequence, wastes time whilst the searcher tries to find a particular part number.

Inventory recording is an essential pre-requisite for the next step, material requirements planning, which is only possible when the inventory recording system has been proven.

MATERIAL REQUIREMENTS PLANNING (MRP)

This is the general term for a set of procedures for the dependent demand situation. The planning of requirements for components and materials based upon the requirements for higher level assemblies. The master schedule is 'exploded' or 'extended' by the use of bills of materials information and the results are 'netted' against inventory.

Commonly there are two MRP system philosophies, the simpler has already been defined and is frequently offered by manufacturers of the smaller computers with limited internal memory and limitations on back-up storage such as disc or cassette devices. Some of the smaller independent software houses also offer such systems. In the correct context (i.e. certain types of manufacturing contract work) the approach produces an acceptable solution. The principal limitation is that it ignores time, which has two main disadvantages:

1. Inventory is increased because items are ordered into stock before they are actually required. This causes accountants to become concerned over liquidity and has been known to result in directives from chief executives to reduce inventory which often damages the company more than the holding of excessive inventory

2. Production delays caused by stock-outs. These arise when requirements have been netted off against outstanding orders which had later delivery dates than the original acceptable date for the requirement. Again the consequences are costly and much effort is expended in recriminations, alibis and similar unproductive work

The second and more satisfactory version of MRP philosophy is time series planning. This offers a better solution to the manufacturer who finances his own inventory and has to compromise between inventory cost and inventory turnover, and production technique. He anticipates demand, which is expressed in terms of quantity and date, and this is organised into specific time periods (days, weeks, fortnights, months etc.) as appropriate to the business. Order release dates are based on the anticipated inventory which will be on hand in future time periods. As the available inventory is reduced by netting off the requirement, order release dates are determined from lead times and the appropriate 'offset' is calculated to identify when order action needs to be taken.

The above is only an outline of the MRP framework; to add substance to the framework there follows a description of an actual example of such a system in the form it exists at the time of writing.

The management required a system which would look forward 18×4-weekly periods in 'time buckets' of two weeks each. The system would differentiate between A, B and C inventory classification based on value of annual usage. Rules for order quantities were to be provided to deal with a wide range of purchasing and made-in-works batch sizes. The system would also have the capability of handling contract work where the prime criterion was meeting the delivery date and for which the customer would finance the inventory, also handling 'private venture' products which conform to the standard inventory/time constraints.

A further requirement was the facility to allocate any item to the assembly or project with the highest present priority, irrespective of the reason the item was originally requisitioned, and have the system recommend the appropriate remedial materials ordering and re-scheduling action. Finally, the capability of handling embodiment loan items was required.

The course of action adopted was to use IBM's requirements planning package. One small product group was chosen to be the pilot project for testing out the system. This was selected for the following reasons:

a. The product was established and accurately documented

b. The range was small enough to be readily manageable if it became necessary to revert to the manual system whilst dealing with unexpected problems

c. The product used almost all the materials planning facilities specified and would thoroughly test the system except in respect of data volumes

The items in the product group were reviewed and given the inventory classifications 'A' or 'C'. Over several years' running experience only these two classifications have ever been used in the system.

The 'production plan' or master schedule was initiated and included a feature in which management would authorise the purchase of materials and components for a specified amount of a product.

The batching rules available were most comprehensive, they included:

Discrete: 'one for one' which is used for expensive items

Fixed batch: items which have to be manufactured in set quantities due to technical process constraints

These rules are selected by a code for each item within the part number master file.

The system was initiated using lead times based on the experience of the buyers and production control staff. However, within months problems developed which were diagnosed as the result of inaccurate lead times. It was found impractical to have the buyer update the lead time each time an order was placed and in practice the delivery promises made by suppliers are not always reliable, especially when the national economy surges. The remedial action was to set up a sub-system which measured the actual elapsed time between placing an order and receipt of the goods. (A shop order does not differ from a purchase order, except for the supplier, as far as this aspect is concerned.) The monitor system checks if the lead time variance exceeds a tolerance parameter. When lead time increases, the lead time field of the part master record

(PNMF) is changed to the new actual lead time. A report is made to the purchasing department of these changes showing old and new lead times. The buyer can override the calculated figure when necessary.

When the lead time is reduced, the change is reported to the buyer by the system which will continue to use the old lead time unless the buyer confirms the change.

Two 'requirements planning' modules are used: the most important is requirements generation which is initiated by loading the master schedule (production plan). The system initially deletes all gross requirements and planned orders leaving only the open order information. The master schedule is loaded into the gross requirement for the appropriate time period. Then, starting with the highest level (usually finished products), the system reviews what inventory is available to meet the requirement, taking into account any open orders due for delivery in that time period and any allocations and assignments made for previously released issue instructions. If there is a surplus availability of inventory of the item, this is carried forward into the next time period. This continues until either all requirements in the planning horizon are met or a net requirement results. This net requirement is then 'lot sized' in accordance with the prescribed rule for the item, and then offset in time (backward scheduling) by the lead time, thus identifying the 'time bucket' in which the requisition for the item must be initiated.

When the item is an assembly (and is not a raw material or purchased item) the system explodes each planned order into its constituent parts, extends the quantity per unit shown on the bill of materials file, adjusts for scrap allowance and loads the resulting requirements into the gross requirement balance of the appropriate time bucket.

The system repeats this action for all items having 'low level code O' (i.e. finished stock) and only when all the items at that level have been dealt with does the system repeat the process for the items at level 1 then, similarly, progresses through the succeeding lower level items until raw materials and purchase parts have been scheduled.

The system recognises purchased items and raw materials by their type code which signifies that a product structure (bill of materials) will not be called up and exploded.

The second materials planning module is 'a net change system' which in principle works as does the requirements generation module except that it handles only changes and does not set all gross requirement and planned order balances to zero when initiated. This is useful where the rate of change of end product requirement is moderate as it reduces the computer run time required. We regard it as supplementary to but not replacing the full requirement generation system.

There are two principal results from the requirements planning systems, these are (i) requisitions, and (ii) exception notices. Although much of the essential information to initiate a purchase requisition is available, on the requirements generation report, if such a report were printed for an inventory of thousands of items it would be extremely unwieldy. In practice it is edited and made available to production control and purchasing departments in manageable form on a visual display terminal or as a list of requisitions if on-line facilities are not used.

The program producing these requisitions scans the results of the material requirements planning process and searches for planned orders. It looks ahead only for a limited period (say four or eight weeks) set by a parameter specified for each run by production control staff. In practice it was found that to look further ahead, the frequency of order changes was unacceptable. When the planned orders were abstracted, the work file was sorted to produce separate reports for purchase items and made-in-works items. In fact the sort segregated the information for each buyer or production control scheduler who received an action report of the products for which he was responsible. The requisition list also contains warning messages for buyers that changes of programme have resulted in a requirement inside the normal lead time and gives the specific quantity urgently required.

Exception notices are printed when conditions are found in the materials requirements planning process which infringe the framework on which the system is predicated. This can be illustrated by considering the situation which arises when a finished product is scheduled for delivery well inside its standard lead time and where the 'in-process' inventory does not 'buy enough time' to meet the required delivery promised. The MRP system will progressively back-schedule assemblies offsetting from the delivery date and will at various stages encounter requirements which should have been met before today's date. The system logic is that 'yesterday cannot be changed' and consequently it schedules the requirement into the current time period (MRP does not consider shop or supplier capacity) and 'flags' the requirement with an appropriate exception condition code.

At the end of the MRP process the number of reports of each exception type are summarised by VDU or in printed form for each production scheduler's attention.

PURCHASING

The use of computers in purchase ledger work was another of their early applications. A computer can, of course, reproduce purchase requisitions as purchase orders, particularly for repeat orders. However, it is often advantageous to interpose buying skill and judgement when placing orders based on requisitions.

The purchase orders are an important part of the production control function and consequently are included as part of the computer system. One of the most practical methods of holding purchase order information is to create an open order file as a subordinate part master file associated with the PNMF. The PNMF is accessed by reference to the part numbers and identifies the record address of the first open order record for the part on the subordinate part master file. As records are added to the subordinate file the records referring to the same part number are 'chained' together i.e. each record contains fields which identify the location of preceding and succeeding records.

The open order file can and usually does refer to both internal works orders and purchase orders, and is maintained by processing;

a. New orders

b. Order changes (quantity, delivery dates etc.)

c. Order cancellations

d. Goods received

e. Goods accepted

It is advisable to consider the information required for these transactions carefully and relate this to the design and distribution of both the purchase order form and the goods receiving notes.

The information on the open purchase order file is used by the materials requirements planning system as previously described and additionally provides purchase order action information, individual purchase order action notes, and project purchase order situation reports. This type of status reporting (on printed lists or VDU display) replaces the detailed clerical work of writing up deliveries on purchase order progress reports. The value lies in the fact that all the orders requiring attention are notified for the management's attention. More sophisticated systems use the same information to update the supplier (vendor) master records on which vendor performance rating systems are based. The extent of information held on the supplier master file is dependent on the degree of sophistication of the system. In practice it is found in both factoring and manufacturing businesses that supplier information is most valuable.

The decision whether to use batch processing or on-line techniques with VDU equipment is not easy. Purchasing accounts for major expenditure and it has a strong economic case for the necessary resources being allocated. It has been demonstrated that a buyer using VDU equipment calling up information from stock, supplier, product structure and requirements planning files increases his efficiency in minimising production delays due to stock-outs (e.g. the use of alternate materials) and in his negotiating and placing of orders. This information can, of course, be made available by 'batch' systems provided the time lag is acceptable.

The necessity of processing goods received notes to maintain stock records and open order status records introduces the possibility of using the same information in cost and purchase ledger accounting. In such a system the GRN can be used to maintain a purchase reserve file, to produce purchase variance reports, and for input to the purchase ledger and purchase analyses systems.

KITTING AND RELEASING

The elements of production control discussed above are concerned with the provisioning of materials i.e. planning for the future material needs weeks or months in advance of the requirement. This section deals with the action necessary when components and materials are required for the shop floor.

The trigger mechanism necessary to initiate production control's requests for components or materials is frequently the made-in-works requisition produced by the MRP system. Production control should, prior to creating the works order documentation, confirm that the requisite materials and components are available. The principle can be illustrated by considering the situation of an assembly shop making variable size batches of a number of different assemblies.

The production scheduler concerned (despatcher) needs to know if the components required are available and if not, the stock and on-order situation. He states certain conditions:

1. Batch quantity required

2. Issue date required (when the batch is to be issued to shop)

3. Quantity tolerance (would a 10% reduction of batch size be acceptable?)

4. Should forward deliveries be included in availability lists?

5. Priority indicator

The computer system sorts the request for batches into the priority sequence specified by the scheduler to ensure the batches of greatest priority have first call on available components, then it calls up the product structure (single level) of the assembly and extends the quantity required of each component by the batch quantity. Scrap allowance may or may not be included as specified in each situation. The extended requirement is first reviewed for mandatory items (e.g. a printed circuit board may be mandatory but a component on that board not mandatory). Availability of the mandatory items is first checked since shortages of such items (which are essential to starting assembly work) mean either a reduction in batch quantity released or the prevention of the release due to shortage. The non-mandatory items are next checked for availability.

a. *Release*: when availability of components permits, a picking or kitting list is produced for the released batch. The quantity of each component allocated to the batch are added to the allocation field in the PNMF record for the component thus modifying the availability when the next batch is processed

b. *Shortage*: if the availability situation precludes the release of the kit as specified, the request is flagged and bypassed until all batches which can be released have been dealt with. A shortage report is produced for each unsuccessful kit request. This identifies all components required showing the required quantity, availability and the outstanding orders

CAPACITY PLANNING

Production control are concerned with the production capacity of the factory in addition to the materials planning in order to control the factory's production. Success in the use of computing depends on management recognising the real requirements. The solution for in-flow line work, e.g. a steel works, is very different from a batch process, e.g. a press shop or machine shop. For products which have very short process times or are in continuous production, on-line data collection equipment usually is required, whereas in the batch production situation with long cycle times the response speed is in the order of days or weeks and consequently on-line equipment for progress information is not readily justifiable.

In managing production resources the primary considerations are capacity, load and job sequence. Production managers have to consider, in the case of the first two elements, the appropriate unit of measurement, machine hours or man hours or a mix of both.

The approaches adopted for capacity planning may be simulation for batch manufacturing operations and linear programming for process operations. The linear programming technique is concerned with mathematical modelling to optimise conflicts of interacting resources. Simulation is more frequently used, primarily because the majority of manufacturing processes are based on batch production. Computer simulation requires three main files:

Work centre master file

Routing file

Work-in-progress file

The work centre master file contains records for each machine or group of like machines, and for each work-centre capacity values are specified; these may be hours, machine hours or man hours. Variations in capacity at different dates (to cater for scheduled maintenance etc.) are created within a shop calendar. If appropriate, alternative work centres can be specified to permit the system to off-load work batches from an overloaded machine or work centre to one which is an alternative.

The routing file is analogous to the product structure file in the materials planning system, in that it consists of chains of linked records defining the process steps in manufacturing a component. Each step identifies the work centre on which the operation will be performed and the set-up, run, post-operation and inspection times for a standard batch of the components.

A transit time matrix table can also be specified to cater for inter-shop and inter-plant movement of work batches.

The work-in-progress (WIP) file consists of records of batches of work which have been released to the shop but not completed or have been cancelled.

The procedure adopted in capacity planning is first to identify run date within the shop calendar and thence to determine what capacity is available for each work centre.

The system uses a technique based on (i) infinite capacity backward scheduling, and (ii) infinite capacity forward scheduling.

The first case starts with the due date for the finished batch of work and loads the appropriate time value against the final work centre involved then, allowing for transit time and work time, repeats this operation for each preceding operation specified on the routing file.

The second case starts from the current date, loads the first operation on the first work centre and continues loading the sequence of operation on the work centres.

When the results of these two operations are combined with the WIP load, a capacity load profile is calculated showing the over- and under-loads compared to the stated shop capacity.

Subsequent functions are finite capacity scheduling and load smoothing which re-arranges the load into the available capacity taking account of work centre queues and reporting delays. There are a number of functions available within such systems which can compute the result of splitting batches, job overlapping, transit time reduction, alternative machine centres and alternative routings. The new user would be well advised to start with a minimum of parameters until he is sure he understands the composite effects.

Job sequencing attempts to optimise the sequence in which batches are processed on work centres. However, this approach is not strongly favoured, it being considered more practical to leave sequencing to shop supervision.

Capacity planning systems provide management with a very powerful planning tool. Frequently it is not practical to change shop capacity on a day-to-day basis. Therefore, commonly, information is most useful in planning several weeks or months ahead in order to cater for potential overload situations. Reports are prepared of the long- and medium-term to plan for new machines or re-engineered manufacturing methods.

The system can be used by a manufacturer who produces to contract to simulate the load situation which would result were further contracts added to the current load.

In the working environment it is important that the 'system credibility' is upheld and an essential aspect of this is to link the availability of materials and tools and use realistic starting dates for the loading procedure. It is pointless to load a batch of work at a starting date prior to the date when the requisite materials are available, since the result would be a work-to list and a load which are not practical. It is possible to link materials planning and capacity planning systems and exchange information between the two—however we would counsel a cautious approach, using a limited linkage with close manual control in any but the most expertly managed system.

There are particular practical problems in producing and controlling shop floor documentation, drawings, layouts, job tickets, with this type of system. In small and medium-sized enterprises this is usually a 'paper-work' function handled within the production control function. In larger plants with greater complexity and more resources it is possible to provide shop floor control using on-line computer terminals to maintain a data base to minimise the volume of paper on the shop floor. Such systems will provide progress, machine status, load and capacity information. Senior management must be cautious in their use of such facilities as the availability of such information can induce over-reaction.

Index